Customized Job Training for Business and Industry

Robert J. Kopecek, Robert G. Clarke, *Editors*

NEW DIRECTIONS FOR COMMUNITY COLLEGES
Sponsored by the ERIC Clearinghouse for Junior Colleges
ARTHUR M. COHEN, *Editor-in-Chief*
FLORENCE B. BRAWER, *Associate Editor*

Number 48, December 1984

Paperback sourcebooks in
The Jossey-Bass Higher Education Series

Jossey-Bass Inc., Publishers
San Francisco • Washington • London

EDUCATIONAL RESOURCES INFORMATION CENTER

Clearinghouse For Junior Colleges

UNIVERSITY OF CALIFORNIA, LOS ANGELES

Robert J. Kopecek, Robert G. Clarke (Eds.).
Customized Job Training for Business and Industry.
New Directions for Community Colleges, no. 48.
Volume XII, number 4.
San Francisco: Jossey-Bass, 1984.

New Directions for Community Colleges Series
Arthur M. Cohen, *Editor-in-Chief*; Florence B. Brawer, *Associate Editor*

New Directions for Community Colleges (publication number USPS 121-710)
is published quarterly by Jossey-Bass Inc., Publishers, in association with
the ERIC Clearinghouse for Junior Colleges. *New Directions* is numbered
sequentially—please order extra copies by sequential number. The volume
and issue numbers above are included for the convenience of libraries.
Second-class postage rates paid at San Francisco, California, and at additional
mailing offices.

The material in this publication was prepared pursuant to a contract
with the National Institute of Education, U.S. Department of Education.
Contractors undertaking such projects under government sponsorship
are encouraged to express freely their judgment in professional and
technical matters. Prior to publication, the manuscript was submitted
to the Center for the Study of Community Colleges for critical review and
determination of professional competence. This publication has met such
standards. Points of view or opinions, however, do not necessarily represent
the official view or opinions of the Center for the Study of Community
Colleges or the National Institute of Education.

Correspondence:
Subscriptions, single-issue orders, change of address notices, undelivered
copies, and other correspondence should be sent to Subscriptions,
Jossey-Bass Inc., Publishers, 433 California Street, San Francisco
California 94104.

Editorial correspondence should be sent to the Editor-in-Chief,
Arthur M. Cohen, at the ERIC Clearinghouse for Junior Colleges,
University of California, Los Angeles, California 90024.

Library of Congress Catalogue Card Number LC 83-82722

International Standard Serial Number ISSN 0194-3081

International Standard Book Number ISBN 87589-990-0

Cover art by Willi Baum
Manufactured in the United States of America

This publication was prepared with funding from the National Institute of
Education, U.S. Department of Education, under contract no. 400-83-0030.
The opinions expressed in the report do not necessarily reflect the posi-
tions or policies of NIE or the Department.

Ordering Information

The paperback sourcebooks listed below are published quarterly and can be ordered either by subscription or single-copy.

Subscriptions cost $35.00 per year for institutions, agencies, and libraries. Individuals can subscribe at the special rate of $25.00 per year *if payment is by personal check.* (Note that the full rate of $35.00 applies if payment is by institutional check, even if the subscription is designated for an individual.) Standing orders are accepted. Subscriptions normally begin with the first of the four sourcebooks in the current publication year of the series. When ordering, please indicate if you prefer your subscription to begin with the first issue of the *coming* year.

Single copies are available at $8.95 when payment accompanies order, and *all single-copy orders under $25.00 must include payment.* (California, New Jersey, New York, and Washington, D.C., residents please include appropriate sales tax.) For billed orders, cost per copy is $8.95 plus postage and handling. (Prices subject to change without notice.)

Bulk orders (ten or more copies) of any individual sourcebook are available at the following discounted prices: 10–49 copies, $8.05 each; 50–100 copies, $7.15 each; over 100 copies, *inquire.* Sales tax and postage and handling charges apply as for single copy orders.

To ensure correct and prompt delivery, all orders must give either the *name of an individual* or an *official purchase order number.* Please submit your order as follows:

Subscriptions: specify series and year subscription is to begin.
Single Copies: specify sourcebook code (such as, CC8) and first two words of title.

Mail orders for United States and Possessions, Latin America, Canada, Japan, Australia, and New Zealand to:
Jossey-Bass Inc., Publishers
433 California Street
San Francisco, California 94104

Mail orders for all other parts of the world to:
Jossey-Bass Limited
28 Banner Street
London EC1Y 8QE

New Directions for Community Colleges Series
Arthur M. Cohen, *Editor-in-Chief*
Florence B. Brawer, *Associate Editor*

Contents

Editors' Notes

Contracted customized training for business and industry is a significant new program focus occurring at community colleges. The programs are being provided for a wide variety of firms as a result of a combination of social and economic forces at work in society for the last decade. This specialized education for the private sector is one of the reasons why community colleges are gaining in stature across the country.

This sourcebook describes and analyzes customized education and training from a number of vantage points. When describing how and what is being done, the varied viewpoints expressed by the contributors illustrate that there is, as yet, no one accepted way to structure or organize a college to most effectively offer training. What is also clear from the programs described is that local needs and conditions within the community to be served and within the college providing the program dictate most strongly what and how successful programs are offered. The development of customized education and training is following the strong community college tradition of meeting local and regional needs with uniquely local solutions.

Chapters One, Two, Three, and Eight deal with the definition, organization, and delivery of programs. Kopecek, in Chapter One, defines and describes customized training and presents an integrated organizational model. Connor, on the other hand, in Chapter Three, argues strongly that a centralized organizational structure staffed by generalists produces the best results. In Chapter Two, Clarke compares and contrasts several aspects of the training function with traditional credit programs, and Kaplan in Chapter Eight delineates components necessary for the successful program implementation.

Chapters Four, Five, and Six describe significantly different but successful training programs being offered in three different states. Owen, in Chapter Five, presents a detailed statement of the North Carolina training system implemented over the last twenty years. This historically developed presentation illustrates what can be done with strong, enlightened governmental support at the state level. In Chapter Four, Day outlines a cooperative program, worked out by the college and a major producer of basic metals. Of note is the emphasis in this program on utilizing the DACUM approach to curriculum development. McGuire, in Chapter Six, describes legislative, corporate, and educational cooperation that has allowed the thirty community colleges

1

of New York State to emerge as economic development forces in their communities to foster increased productivity and an approved economic climate.

Finally, Luther, in Chapter Seven, gives an industrial perspective to customized job training and emphasizes training as the correct response to the Japanese influence and the information age. He outlines how educators should interact with business and industry and urges cooperation.

Robert J. Kopecek
Robert G. Clarke
Editors

Robert J. Kopecek is president of Northampton County Area Community College in Pennsylvania.

Robert G. Clarke is president of Vermont Technical College, Randolph Center, Vermont.

*Providing customized job training presents problems as well
as opportunities to the community college. The issues to
be considered in deciding whether a college should become
involved in industrial training are discussed, and
an organizational model for delivering such programs
successfully is suggested.*

Customized Job Training: Should Your Community College Be Involved?

Robert J. Kopecek

American firms spend between $30 billion and $100 billion yearly on the training and education of employees. By comparison, approximately $50 billion is expended annually on all other aspects of higher education (Boyer, 1983). These huge expenditures for training illustrate the growing conviction among business leaders that ongoing education and training of employees are necessary for profitability.

According to Edgerton (1983, p. 4), "by 1990 ten to fifteen million manufacturing workers will no longer be needed in the jobs they now have. With the baby-boom generation reaching maturity, far fewer people will be entering the labor force afresh. Eighty-five to 90 percent of the labor force of 1990 is already in place." These facts, added to the current volume of training across the nation, "establish the parameters of an adult-retraining problem (or opportunity) of immense proportion."

While most industrial instruction is now offered by in-house trainers or consulting firms, many businesses are beginning to contract

R. Kopecek, R. Clarke (Eds.). *Customized Job Training for Business and Industry.*
New Directions for Community Colleges, no. 48. San Francisco: Jossey-Bass, December 1984.

for these kinds of programs from community colleges. The firms are finding the instruction and support services excellent and the prices competitive. The colleges are discovering that industrial instruction is complementary to their other programs and a logical extension of their mission. Such instruction is also proving to be an important factor in the economic vitality of some regions, and it has, for colleges, the added advantage of enhancing their status with business in the community.

Many community college leaders, therefore, are deciding whether conditions are right in their community and at their college to enter the industrial training field. Questions abound: For example, is it wise, when colleges are facing serious financial and enrollment problems and when the current mix of instruction is already cited as over-emphasizing the career and vocational, to focus more staff and resources on customized training for business and industry? The opportunity to provide a needed educational service directly to industry, a market segment that has great financial resources, high potential need, and much political influence, is very tempting, but there are real risks — philosophical, organizational, and financial.

This chapter suggests issues of concern for community college officials facing the questions of whether and to what extent their college should pursue the industrial training market, and it discusses the advantages and disadvantages of this type of involvement.

A Description of Customized Job Training

Customized (tailored) industrial training is defined as training that is designed to meet the specific and unique task or skill needs of a particular firm. Vocational programs are usually short, less than forty hours in length, while technical or management programs may be over 120 hours in duration. The instruction is narrow in technical orientation; it focuses on skills and usually is based on a task analysis of jobs already in existence.

The students enrolled are either new employees, who require entry-level skills or specific orientation to processes and techniques of the firm, or continuing employees who need upgrading or retraining because of promotion, technological change, or basic changes in the company's operations.

The training may occur in the workplace, in a traditional educational setting, or in a combination of both. The instructional program is designed, organized, and administered by the personnel of the college with the direct assistance of individuals from the industry. The instruction is actually provided by individuals recruited (and trained if necessary), employed, and supervised by the college. The faculty may be full-time teaching staff of the college or, more likely, are specially recruited practitioners or trainers who know the industry in question and can relate well to corporate goals and objectives.

Initial Concerns

What Are Local Needs and Attitudes? For college personnel contemplating offering industrial training, the answers to questions regarding probable need and utilization are central. Do area businesses and industries need and want training? Are area firms retooling, planning to produce new product lines, establishing plants, or hiring new personnel? Do area firms recognize the need for ongoing training for all of their employees, and are these firms prepared to contract for this service?

Before a college commits to industrial training, market research is required. A systematic needs analysis of the community, for example, is essential. Entering the industrial training field in a substantial manner most likely will require a restructuring of the college's internal operations to accommodate this new form of instruction. If the predicted need for training, based on market research, is significant, then the college can make the necessary changes more confidently. (Possible organizational changes are discussed later in this chapter.)

Colleges discovering marginal need, however, are wise to accommodate occasional requests for training on an incidental, case-by-case basis and not to alter their basic organizational style or mode of operation. The specific results from market research needed by a college before it can commit to establishing special arrangements for the offering of contracted services will vary, but positive responses from at least ten firms requiring at least $100,000 to $250,000 worth of training during a year seem a reasonable minimum. The dollar range is wide because costs differ greatly depending on the type and sophistication of training required, the amount of equipment needed, and the availability and cost of competent instructors.

When the initial need is predicted to be great, the college should raise other questions. How comprehensive can the college be? What are the perceptions of the community and the college's sponsors relative to training as an aspect of the college's mission? Will aggressive efforts in training be viewed as consistent with the mission of the college, or will it cause widespread misunderstandings? People who believe that public money should not be used to assist any profit-making organization directly may oppose vigorously and vocally any efforts by a public college to provide corporate training, even though all costs can be demonstrated to be carried by the private-sector company. Public acceptance of the training role of public institutions for the private sector is a recent phenomenon.

Faculty Attitudes. Faculty and staff, also, may not be willing to accept the extension of the college's mission and philosophy to include extensive industrial training. Some may fear that it may tarnish the hard-won status of the college in the higher education community. The instruction may not be perceived as being on a collegiate level.

Perhaps a more serious problem is faculty opposition to the expansion of customized job training (CJT) programs on the grounds of economic timeliness. They may argue that the concept is valid but that, given decreasing funds available per student from all sources, extending CJT capacity will simply drain off resources from existing and more traditional programs. It should be recognized that if CJT programs are appropriately administered and priced, no college needs to subsidize them beyond some relatively small start-up costs. In fact, industrial training should more than pay for itself after the first six months of extensive programming.

Changing the Focus of the Instructional Process. Most programs regularly offered by community colleges focus on meeting the educational goals and objectives of individuals as identified and defined by those individuals. And the individuals who enroll in a college's program of study assume that knowledgeable professionals have developed the curriculum with both the students' needs and high educational standards in mind. Each of these situations is perfectly normal for the academic institution providing quality education in traditional settings. However, involvement in industrial training threatens both circumstances by changing the focus of education in two ways. First, the college's program integrity may be affected by the attempt to satisfy the needs of the firm requiring training; second, the motivation of the student in the industrial training program is changed.

The name, customized job training, implies that the training program is specifically designed for the contracting firm. Therefore, the personnel of the firm must work with the college staff in designing programs that fit the firm's objectives. The danger is that, in the attempt to tailor the program to the firm, the firm may be allowed to exercise too much control over the scope and content of the program, with the result that focus is shifted away from basic principles of quality education. Faculty and administration of the college must be alert to maintaining program integrity even though the firm, a paying client, may be more interested in results than in procedure. To ignore this potential area of concern is to threaten the academic reputation of the college.

For the student of regular college programs, the motivation to attend and succeed at a course of study arises from the individual's interests, perceptions, and objectives. The arrangements for offering the course, the content of the course, the techniques of instruction, and the financial arrangements are typically worked out between the student and the college. Clearly, the needs, desires, and interests of the individual student are a primary focus of the college. When a third party, in the form of the contracting firm, is introduced into this arrangement, a change necessarily occurs. Although the basic focus of concern is and must remain on the learning needs of the students, the client of the college (and the entity paying the bill) is the firm contracting for the instruction. As already mentioned, personnel of the firm will be directly involved in determining the contents of the course and, ultimately, in evaluating the course in terms of how well the material taught is applicable to the workplace. The firm will decide who needs the course, who will attend the training programs. This removes from the individual student the intrinsic motivational asset of determining his or her own educational goals and the path that he or she should take to achieve them. This altered pattern is psychologically destructive for some students.

There may also be great differences in the interests as well as abilities of students who attend the program. Instructors in CJT need to be highly competent in their fields, but they must also be familiar with the techniques of the specific industry involved if they are to succeed in coping with informed questions and a high skill level from motivated veteran practitioners. On the other hand, although by no means the rule, some employees may be enrolled in courses against their will and asked to learn skills and adapt to attitudes that may not interest them. The problems inherent in teaching such students are not unlike those encountered with the unmotivated, traditional eighteen-year-old student, but the techniques used to overcome the problems may be very different. Further, if the instruction is conducted on site in a manufacturing plant, plant supervisors may interfere by being more interested in short-term production deadlines than in the long-term benefits that accrue to employees and the firm as a result of systematic employee participation in training programs. All such differences of opinion regarding objectives, contents, values, and results of customized training programs must be overcome if meaningful training is to occur.

CJT is a type of instruction with which most community colleges have had at least some experience, but, as the magnitude of such programming increases, the unique instructional issues, along with obvious differences in course identification and administration, must be worked out.

Personnel Implications. Essential to effective CJT programming is a cadre of knowledgeable and committed individuals. These staff members must know their college, be able to conceptualize quickly and easily the potential training needs of industry, and have the ability to market, develop, and implement training programs. Effective programming is closely tied to the caliber of people with these talents who can be identified from among current staff or employed specifically for this function. Whatever organizational structure is used to implement training programs the involved staff must be identified clearly, must internalize its function, and must have clear policies and procedures that make it bureaucratically simple to deliver the training. The staff must know that CJT is an institutional priority supported by senior college officials if the training effort is to succeed.

The college must further have the reputation of delivering what it promises. It must, therefore, stand behind any commitments made by the staff. CJT programming is conducted outside of the college with firms who operate in a milieu much different from the traditional academic world. Boundaries of individual authority must be known clearly to CJT staff and to their colleagues at the college. Who is entitled to commit the college to how much must be understood explicitly. This is not to imply that any individual calling on business firms or implementing training contracts must be able to draw up or sign contracts on the spot. Except for very small businesses, most corporate executive officers do not have this type of authority! What is important, however, is to have staff members who can correctly commit the college and who can accurately estimate costs.

Institutional integrity must be preserved, but an entrepreneurial style is essential. Entrepreneurship is an atypical attribute for most individuals currently employed in education, but that is the nature of CJT activities. The honest tension between institutional integrity and entrepreneurship must be acknowledged. Staff members must recognize that they are selling their programs in a competitive market. Business people expect a fair presentation of a potential program, but they will attempt to get as much as possible for their money. College personnel, further, need to recognize that more than money can be at stake.

Most simply stated, what is required to maximize CJT programming are capable people operating in a sound and workable organizational structure that makes sense within the context of the particular college. The structure must allow and facilitate talented and trained people to focus on the task of delivering high-quality, low-cost, specialized instruction.

The Integrated Model

If CJT is to become a significant portion of the total work load of an institution, it may be necessary to restructure the organization. Most colleges cannot expand their efforts into contracted services and continue to provide quality instruction in other degree programs while conducting business as usual. CJT programming will have implications for virtually every administrative area in the college with an especially strong impact on instruction. The integrated model outlined in this section suggests one approach to coping with the needed changes.

This model holds that the best people available in any college to contact, set up, teach, and administer training programs are those same administrators and faculty who offer preservice education in the same discipline. For example, if a company requires its draftspersons and design engineers to be trained in computer-aided design/computer-assisted manufacturing (CAD/CAM), individuals from the drafting and design departments of the college are in the best position to offer or supervise in-service instruction. In like manner, if office personnel require training in word processing, who could be better suited to meet this need than individuals from the secretarial science department of the college?

The integrated model establishes an organizational structure and policies and procedures that encourage the interaction of faculty and staff who possess specific disciplinary expertise with their counterparts in business and industrial firms. This approach has at least two major benefits: It encourages faculty and staff related to every career and technical program at the college to assume responsibility for the in-service as well as preservice education and training offered, and it fosters decentralized decision making.

From a curricular viewpoint, the integrated approach vertically organizes the college. One group of faculty and one academic administrator are responsible for all instruction offered at the college in a particular discipline. The approach recognizes that the emphasis placed on "credit" as opposed to "noncredit" instruction is a reflection of the views of professors and not of practitioners or their employers. Practitioners want only new skills or knowledge in order to cope with changes in their fields. The approach recognizes further that, because of the nature of preservice education, the contents of some noncredit courses, which reflect the newest trends in an industry, are the most advanced offered at the institution — although these courses cannot be applied to any degree offered by the college.

This point is illustrated by a CJT course offered at the request of a hospital to registered nurses (RNs) on new developments in nursing practice. All of the students in this noncredit course, which is not applicable to a degree, are licensed RNs who have already completed successfully the preservice program and are now working. These individuals need new skills that may not be taught in the preservice curriculum. Who at a college should work with the director of nursing services at the contracting hospital in developing the training program? Who should develop the curriculum and even teach this course? The most logical person is the college's director of nursing! No other individual, surely no other college administrator trained as a generalist, knows the subject or the peculiarities of the workplace as well. No other individual is likely to be as capable of developing curriculum and of knowing individuals who have the requisite skills to teach the course.

The integrated model also uses the best available personnel at the college for outreach into the community. Community college faculty members are technically very competent, but, unfortunately, in most communities this reserve of human capital is not adequately recognized and may even be overlooked. CJT gives college faculty and staff a direct method of preparing individuals to be more productive, and it allows them to share their technical as well as pedagogical skills and knowledge with colleagues in business.

The integrated model also gives long-time administrators and faculty members of career and technical programs the opportunity to interact professionally with the employers of their preservice students on a new level. It allows, perhaps even forces, the college-bound academic administrator and faculty member to get into the field. This process benefits the college, for it updates personnel. But, more important for successful CJT programs, these educators provide tremendous assistance to individuals in the workplace.

The integrated model further guards against the unwanted development at a college of two different and distinct faculties in the same discipline. These faculties are composed of traditional professors, who hold full-time tenure-track positions and teach preservice students, and trainers, who are usually part-time adjunct instructors less familiar with the college, who teach credit-free training programs.

This organizational pattern also helps to ensure increased curricular control and a standardization of students' performance expectations by providing the opportunity for full-time faculty involvement and the supervision of all instruction within a discipline by the same administrative officer.

The integrated model is not a panacea. Full-time faculty, because of their commitment to preservice programs, often do not have the time for or the interest in CJT programs. To some, the prospect of training is even threatening, for it is a very different approach to instruction. But, if they can be motivated to become involved and if it can be scheduled, full-time faculty members can make very valuable contributions to short-term, quickly conceived, training programs. There are further strong curriculum and instructional benefits for both in-service and preservice programs if all of the instruction in a discipline is the responsibility of one administrator.

If a college accepts the logic of an integrated approach for CJT programming, the same logic extends to all instruction. While reflecting a strong commitment to the concept of continuing education and lifelong learning, the integrated approach calls into question the need for a separate continuing education organizational unit with its own staff, budget, policies, and procedures and with its tendency to emphasize dichotomies between credit and noncredit programs, courses, and faculty.

To make the integrated model work, academic program administrators need to broaden their professional concerns beyond the scope of preservice programs. Deans and program directors must alter their priorities. Methods of administering and managing must be adapted to ensure that all of the productive time of these academic administrators is not consumed by the demands of preservice programs. Furthermore, a more entrepreneurial attitude needs to be nurtured. Academic administrators need to become much more oriented to the world outside the college, which will increase the probability of extensive CJT programming, and also make college personnel much more sensitive to the divergent attitudes and needs in the community. If guided properly, increased entrepreneurship can stimulate increased excitement among staff members and ultimately improve overall operations.

Using this model, a college is represented in the business and industrial community not just by the president and personnel from the continuing education office but rather by the president and *every* academic dean, program director, and interested technical faculty member at the institution. The message that customized job training is a college commitment then becomes clear.

Advantages of CJT Programs

Initial concerns aside, there are many potential advantages for the college that becomes involved in providing industrial training programs. The following subsections describe the benefits of such programs to both the college and the community it serves.

12

The Mission of the College. Training specialized for business and industry is an expression of the comprehensive mission of the college and is a function that the college is uniquely capable of offering. CJT is another way for the college to serve taxpayers in a cost-effective way.

Economic Revitalization. Customized job training is an indispensable aspect of economic revitalization efforts. The involvement of the local community college in its community as the deliverer of industrial training has the potential not only of providing well-trained workers but also of developing and cementing relationships between the college and area firms. For regions hard hit by the competitive disadvantage of their products in national and world markets, the establishment of new firms and the extensive product diversification by existing firms are absolute necessities. Changes of this kind require tremendous effort. Not only will affected industry have to develop new products and new methods of production, accumulate sufficient capital for new equipment and plants, and, in many localities, retrofit or build new multipurpose work centers but, most important for community colleges, the retraining of personnel also becomes essential. Since CJT can be offered at a competitive price through the community college, it allows a company to maintain and/or enhance its viability and profitability in the marketplace. In turn this has a positive effect on the local market.

Relationships Between Business and College. By providing training to a business, a college has the potential of creating an entirely different relationship among the personnel of both organizations. The fact that college personnel are working on state-of-the-art problems can dispel notions of the existence of an ivory-tower mentality. Both business and college personnel have a first-hand opportunity to observe each other at work. The residual effects in the community are significant. A prime example is the increased possibility of the firm employing graduates of the college. The relationship may also cause the company to be more generous in responding to the college's needs.

Professional Development of Staff. The involvement of college faculty and staff in problems of local businesses provides an opportunity for professional development of the highest order. It allows college and business staffs with common interests to become professionally acquainted. Further, faculty observing changes in business or industrial practices can, on a first-hand basis, assess the true importance of preservice degree curricula taught at the college. It allows faculty members the opportunity to update their skills and knowledge.

Increased Use of the College. Participation in training programs by corporate employees will demonstrate community college services to yet another segment of the population. If industrial and business employees receive excellent job-related instruction taught by competent and caring individuals in programs administered by the college, the probability is great that these employees will use the college again themselves and pass on their positive feelings to other potential students in their families, their neighborhoods, and in the business community.

Expanded Access to Additional Education. Customized job training can be the beginning of an even more intensive learning process for some individuals. It can have the effect of orienting the individuals toward systematic instruction. It can help them recognize other potentials they may have and can stimulate them to enroll in additional courses or programs. It can put to rest the myth that "older" individuals cannot learn new things.

Personalized College Services for Student-Employees. The individual experiencing successful training benefits directly from the community college can personalize how the college assists people and the community. The successfulness clearly reinforces how the college helped the student-employees, their fellow workers, their company, and their community.

Financially Beneficial. Well administered and properly priced training programs can be lucrative for community colleges. Businesses and industries are accustomed to expending large sums of money to purchase training. CJT programs offered at community colleges can easily be priced at a level to exceed costs substantially while still remaining competitive. In fact, the college may have to overcome the concern of some corporate managers that quality cannot be obtained at prices as low as those commonly established for CJT.

Increased Student-Employee Productivity. The effect of customized job training on the individual student-employee can be very significant. The programs provide the students with the opportunity to learn skills and/or attitudes that will make them immediately more productive at their jobs.

Availability of Government Funding. Because of the recognized need to diversify business and industry and to create new jobs for unemployed and underemployed individuals, several states have established special economic development programs that fund programs for training personnel in new or expanding firms. A community college can serve as an aggressive agent in attempting to link qualified firms to the state and federal funding programs designed to enhance economic development. Although public funding is not an essential ingredient of customized job training, as is evidenced by the amount of money being expended by business for training, the incentive of subsidized training may be a deciding factor to a firm seeking a locality for its operation.

14

Potential Problems

Colleges that become deeply involved with customized job training need to consider the potential problems described in the paragraphs that follow.

Program Integrity. A philosophical issue could be the first and most serious concern. Organizational and curricular control is central to the integrity of all colleges. College personnel need to ensure that direct or subtle pressures by business do not permit the mentality of being "kept" to develop at the college. What is taught and the levels of acceptable achievement must meet defensible educational standards. Colleges should have policies that ensure that the instructional program is not being exploited by any firm; that students are achieving at acceptable levels; and that programs are not pass-throughs for business to obtain governmental largesse.

CJT as a Possible Threat to the College's Comprehensiveness. The amount of training offered by a college can be an issue. College personnel must be concerned with the percentage of the college's total instructional work load devoted to customized job training. That the delivery of this kind of programming will require changes in the college's administrative policies and practices is a given, but the long-term effects of these changes on the essence of the institution are obviously related to the magnitude of the involvement. Most community colleges strive to be comprehensive. Customized job training is likely to exacerbate already changing patterns of student enrollment from degree to short-term programs and from students studying academic subjects to those pursuing technical and vocational offerings.

Failure to Deliver Quality Programming. Finally, the college that offers CJT should recognize that all of the factors that hold tremendous potential for developing positive relationships with business and industry have inherent in them the possibility for exactly the opposite. Firms expend funds for training with the expectation of receiving quality instruction and service. If these services are not delivered to the level of satisfaction advertised and desired, dissatisfaction with the college is bound to result and to be advertised in the community.

References

Boyer, E. L. "Higher Education Should Do More Than Imitate Its Corporate Rivals." *Chronicle of Higher Education,* May 25, 1983, p. 32.
Edgerton, R. "A College Education Up to Beating the Japanese." *AAHE Bulletin,* 1983, *35* (10), 3–7.

Robert J. Kopecek is president of Northampton County Area Community College in Pennsylvania.

The similarities and differences between traditional degree programs and industrial training programs are outlined, and guidelines are presented for the community college entering the industrial training field.

Customized Job Training and Credit Programs

Robert G. Clarke

Although the learning-teaching processes and overall operations are similar in many ways, customized job training and traditional college programming are philosophically and operationally different. This chapter highlights the similarities as well as the differences.

Definitions

Education is the transfer to students of a fundamental base of knowledge that serves as a long-term foundation upon which to grow. Training is "skill-specific" instruction to allow the student to master a defined set of job competencies. *Webster's* (1977) defines education as "the field of study that deals mainly with methods of teaching and learning in schools." Warmbrod and Faddis (1983) define customized job training as either:

1. Short-term customized training for entry-level positions to aid start-up in new or expanding companies, with all or most of the training costs subsidized by the state; or
2. Short- or long-term customized training for upgrading or retraining of extant employees of established companies,

R. Kopecek, R. Clarke (Eds.). *Customized Job Training for Business and Industry.*
New Directions for Community Colleges, no. 48. San Francisco: Jossey-Bass, December 1984.

with occasionally some small subsidies from the state, but most often with training offered to the company at cost by the college.

Averill (1984) notes that "education is now facing the dichotomy of education to serve the student and (or) training which is intended to serve the business community" (p. 34). Goldman and Sutcliffe (1982) state that "education is keyed to drawing out from inside, while instruction is based upon shaping the student from the outside" (p. 3). By substituting the word "training" for "instruction" in the previous sentence, we can identify another operative difference between education and training.

Administrative Response

The amount of administrative time required to integrate industrial training fully into the programmatic offerings of a community college is enormous. This is especially true during the first three to four years of operation while the initial development of the training programs takes place. The strong commitment of senior administrators, which must be communicated to personnel at all levels of the institution, is essential. A college cannot simply hire a director of industrial training and expect that person to establish and implement the program all alone. All levels of administration should be involved in the initial decision-making process that establishes the program, for they surely will be involved in solving the inevitable difficulties that will occur during implementation.

While the process of establishing an associate degree program at a college may involve over the course of an eighteen-month period a few faculty and academic administrators, a lay advisory committee, an assortment of college committees, the president, trustees, and in some states a state agency, the pattern of involvement is usually more complex with training, although the time for participation and decision making may be truncated. The development of a new training program requires the involvement (or at least the acknowledgement) of all of the above people, as well as the guidance and assistance of virtually every other segment of the college's administrative staff on an ongoing basis. (This need for widespread involvement may be a reason that some colleges resist developing these programs fully.)

To ensure this broad-based support, all staff members must understand the needs and objectives of the program. The college may need to reconceptualize and rewrite its mission statement in order to reflect clearly this new manifestation of its continuing education function. This reconceptualization should be endorsed and ratified by the governing board.

A number of possible organizational structures for delivering training are outlined in this book. However, no matter what structure an institution adopts, the institution must see the program as an integral part of its mission, and senior administrators must strongly support and encourage the activity. This point cannot be stressed too much or said too many times. If the president and the board do not make a commitment, customized job training (CJT) will either fail or have limited success. CJT's need for commitment and campuswide support is not dissimilar from the needs of every degree program at the college, but, since large-scale CJT is new, the need is even greater.

Target Group

The college's degree and certificate programs provide preservice education and upgrade training. The individuals enrolled in these programs have decided to go to college to obtain a broad background of knowledge, understandings, and skills (including the ability to find initial employment) or to learn new skills that may provide opportunity for advancement or a change of careers. This population decides to pursue an educational program alone or with the advice of family and friends. While most institutions develop strategic marketing plans to attempt to attract and persuade this type of individual to enroll, it is the individual, independently, who chooses to attend college.

This is not the case in CJT programs. The implications, therefore, on program development, instruction, evaluation, pre- and post-testing, and student performance are enormous. A college's ability to deal with these factors is crucial to success.

It is important to note a subtle but powerful reason why some students may react negatively or with suspicion to CJT programs: The programs are run at the behest of the company!

The following is a scenario that frequently occurs: Someone, probably a supervisor or department manager, identifies a problem. The cause of the problem is traced to improper procedures by line workers, which could be corrected if training were implemented. After receiving corporate approval, the firm's training manager arranges for a community college staff member to meet with company personnel, define the training problem, conceptualize a training solution, identify faculty, define competencies that need to be taught, and develop and schedule the program. Classes begin.

However, from the employees' viewpoint, it is a management

decision to run the training program. Management may not have made clear enough the reason for the program or motivated the workers sufficiently for them to wish to become involved.

Since the focus of planning has been management's, the student-worker's commitment to the training program may not exist. While many community college faculty members extol the virtues of motivated teaching, individuals who have not freely chosen to continue their education and who do not want to be in class can create severe instructional problems.

Motivational techniques to ensure good student performance and satisfaction are clearly needed, and many intrinsic as well as extrinsic reward systems have been used throughout the years. Many companies pay individuals full salaries or time and a half for attending class. A currently popular technique is to tie training into promotions. Students who complete a program successfully are given an increase in salary.

However achieved, the motivation of the worker-student is necessary for success. Adult students taking credit courses for a degree or certificate are often intrinsically motivated. CJT students are more likely to need extrinsic reinforcement. Whatever the motivation—hourly wages, a promotion, a raise upon successful completion of the program, or job retention—it must be made clear to the CJT student-worker why the program is necessary and what the individual will get from it.

Unlike the pattern with students enrolling in credit courses, it is vital that CJT administrative staff and faculty meet with prospective trainees prior to the beginning of classes to help ensure appropriate expectations.

Internal Communications

As in any endeavor, a free and continuous exchange of information within the institution is mandatory if CJT programs are to succeed. Everybody must know what everybody else is doing. Formal meetings or written memorandums can be replaced by hallway dialogue, quick telephone calls, and informal handwritten notes, but the key to success is a constant flow of information about attitudes and feelings as well as data. All parties concerned need to understand the institution's endeavors.

The "chain of command" should not inhibit essential internal dialogue. As emphasized by Peters and Waterman (1982) in *In Search of Excellence,* a constant flow of informal internal communications is prevalent in all successful companies. The same principle operates in community colleges. The director of business and industry programs may be a fourth-tier administrator, reporting to a dean, who reports to the vice-president, who reports to the president. However, a flow of information on an informal, as well as formal basis is required if all levels of administration are to contribute. While this may not be the customary mode of operation at the college, it is critical for CJT programs.

To ensure that everyone — line and staff administrators, faculty, trustees, and support personnel — knows what is happening, CJT administrators should circulate a monthly summary of activities that covers every industry contact. This technique may engender help from unexpected sources.

Faculty

At most colleges, the majority of training programs are taught by adjunct faculty members with current industrial experience. This is not a denigration of full-time faculty, who present excellent instructional programs and are utilized for CJT classes whenever possible. However, industry prefers, if not mandates, a faculty that is not "ivory tower" or theoretical in approach, thinking, or delivery. Instruction needs to be oriented toward application and job relevance. Faculty typically need to have had experience on particular types of equipment or in very specialized operations to be most effective. Usually full-time faculty do not have this directly applicable experience, or their schedule does not permit them to participate.

The process of recruiting adjunct faculty for training does differ from the methods used for credit programs. While formal education is required for all credit faculty, it may not be necessary or appropriate for some business and industry programs. While most adjuncts meet standard educational criteria of credit faculty, some very capable skilled craftspeople who have practiced and perfected their trade and who have a talent and desire to share this experience with others do not possess advanced college degrees. Their talent should be enhanced by special training in pedagogical techniques and used.

A new excellent source of adjunct trainers is the cadre of early retirees from major firms. The depressed economic conditions of the early 1980s have created a pool of highly qualified and talented people. These individuals usually desire only part-time employment and are a definite asset. To ensure that a college has access to these individuals, administrators should maintain ongoing contact with personnel officers of large firms. Ideally, the college would be notified by corporate personnel officers of all early retirees who may be interested in part-time teaching for the college.

However, it is true that, just because someone is a skilled crafts-person or an excellent manager, he or she may not necessarily be a good instructor. All new business and industry instructors need to be given "Train the Trainer" sessions, and college personnel must be available to provide individual assistance on an ongoing basis.

The role of the full-time faculty members, however, should not be overlooked, for they are critical to the success of CJT. Their guidance and knowledge are the backbone for successful business and industry programs even if these faculty members are minimally involved in instruction. Initially, faculty tend to be suspicious of this new service or program and must be oriented to the reasons for the programs and their benefits to the college. Showing faculty how their own degree program is enhanced by CJT — for example, through equipment donations and referrals of students into credit programs — can be persuasive.

Instructional Implications

Task analysis and competency-based vocational education (CBVE) have long been bywords for vocational educators, although the application of these concepts has been spotty throughout the country. While virtually all vocational educators praise these notions and assert that all of their programs are CBVE designed, in fact the concepts are rarely even tried in traditional academic programs. Typically, courses fit into nice, tight blocks of three or four credit hours. Instruction is faculty oriented and each student's skills are not clearly stated upon graduation.

Training must be competency based. An analysis of work problems leads to the development of training programs. A long treatise on developing CBVE programs for business and industry is not needed here, as excellent resource material as available. The DACUM (Developing a Curriculum) approach, for example, which was used with great success by Dundalk Community College in working with the Bethlehem Steel Corporation, is described in detail in another chapter. Suffice it to say that all training should be based upon the actual skills the workers need and not on abstract theoretical knowledge.

To the company whose work force lacks basic skills in reading or mathematics, remedial education is as critical to training as it is in credit programs. Mathematics or reading developmental programs are often needed prior to the initiation of specific job training. Many CJT students have not been to school in twenty years, so remedial education is often helpful in two ways: It allows the individual to gain confidence in his or her ability to learn, and it also is the foundation upon which specific job training can be built.

Training programs tend to be shorter in length than degree or certificate programs. Firms want compressed schedules that take into consideration the work shifts of employees. Some companies want their employees in class for thirty to forty hours per week, while others want classes from midnight to 3 A.M. The college must remain as flexible as possible in order to meet these needs. On the other hand, institutions must be confident enough to tell the company when they cannot meet specific requests. Academic integrity and quality instruction are essential for all programs offered by the college.

The institution must always maintain curricular control. While the needs of the company are of prime import and the institution should accommodate the firm in every way possible, the institution has the responsibility to design and deliver the instructional program and certify its quality.

Program Delivery

Training programs tend to use a different delivery format than traditional college credit courses. For example, in customized management courses, extensive use of role playing and of simulation exercises are of utmost importance.

Technical instruction always has a heavy concentration of "hands-on" exercises. Students need and want active participation and evaluate poorly classes that follow a straight lecture format. The readibility of textbooks must coincide with the abilities of the students, especially in courses that prepare students for entry-level jobs. Handouts and audiovisuals play a key role, and the on-time availability of all items is vital to program success.

Hospitality services are rarely, if ever, utilized in traditional college programs. Many CJT programs require coffee and pastry service in the morning, luncheons, dinners, and other hospitality items. A perfect seminar can be ruined because of a poor meal; thus, this aspect of the program also deserves attention.

Finances

Planning and budgeting for training programs is extremely difficult compared to traditional degree programs. In an ongoing curriculum, a sequence of courses is established with relatively little variation, thereby allowing costs based on a given number of students to be projected. For training, it is difficult to forecast in advance of a fiscal year even the exact number of programs or courses that will be conducted. Typical budgeting and funding mechanisms used by publicly supported colleges, therefore, are not adequate. To overcome this difficulty, many institutions budget a finite amount of money for training as a line item. After the initial start-up, training activities should be at least self-sustaining; it is generally assumed that public money will not be used to maintain these programs.

While credit programs are tuition based and paid for in advance by the student, CJT programs are normally performed according to a contract. Payment may or may not be in advance of training due to the complexities of some corporate billing systems. Many companies will issue a purchase order number and a signed contract for the training program, and then the college must expend its funds for the program prior to receiving payment from the firm. State contracts can be a tremendous problem in this regard. Many states have especially designed state-funded CJT programs for new or expanding firms. However, in Pennsylvania, for example, it can be several months before any payment is received for a project, and significant amounts of institutional funds can be encumbered; this creates cash flow problems to say nothing of the loss of interest on college money.

One advantage of CJT is that it generally requires little capital investment compared to degree programs. Training programs are designed to use existing laboratories or in-plant facilities so that the company's equipment is utilized. However, if specialized equipment is needed and the company's equipment is not available, it usually can be leased easily. If the nature of the training program coincides with other college programs, a possible fringe benefit is the donation of equipment to the college by the firm. This equipment can then be used not only for the CJT program but in other credit courses.

In degree programs, instructional materials and supplies are a significant proportion of the direct expenditures of the college. In CJT programs, on the other hand, the materials and supplies should always be billed as an extra cost item to the firm.

The pricing of training programs is also very different in nature and philosophy from degree programs. Community colleges throughout the nation try to deliver a quality education for the least amount of money. A low tuition or fee proposed to industry can actually jeopardize the chance of the college winning the contract. Higher prices for business and industry programs correlate with industrial pricing, and industry believes you get what you pay for. Strange as it may seem, if community colleges are too inexpensive, industry tends to think the program cannot be good.

If no public money is to be used to subsidize the training, the most common approach to pricing is to determine all anticipated direct costs and then apply, to those direct costs, an indirect rate that has been determined independently based on the costs of institutional overhead. In order to use this approach, the college obviously will need to develop its cost-accounting capabilities, if they do not already exist.

Location

Traditional programs are generally offered on campus. Most CJT programs are conducted on site at the local business or industry. Many industrial employees are afraid of "going to college"; some haven't been to school for twenty or thirty years. Some of this fear can be overcome and the chances of a successful and satisfying training program can be greatly enhanced when classes are held in the plant.

Also, as noted earlier, many programs require specialized equipment that can only be found at the plant. It is costly and foolish to try to duplicate vast amounts of equipment for a training program. Conducting classes on site alleviates these concerns.

For seminar-type presentations, traditional college classrooms equipped with desks are not sufficient. Tables are required, as well as more comfortable seating. Since students enrolled in some intensive training sessions may be in class six hours a day, physical comfort is essential, and other amenities (such as carpeting) to differentiate these rooms from the normal college classroom are desirable. Such considerations are especially important for managers. Professionals desire their continuing education to be conducted in a professional manner and environment.

The Ability to Say No

Telling a company that the college cannot deliver a training program that has been requested is very difficult and is even harder when the college is a fledgling center for business and industry programs. However, the ability to say no will, in reality, help to solidify the institution's place as an industrial trainer.

Institutional integrity must always be maintained, as the long-range success of any program depends upon how well it delivers. The attitude that "anything can be accomplished" is overambitious. There will be occasions when it is in the institution's best interest to say "No, we do not feel that we can deliver a quality program in this area." A short-term loss will be offset by a long-term gain in credibility.

Each program is critical to the overall success of business and industry training. If the college has one or two colossal failures, the entire CJT operation will suffer. The balance between aggressive salesmanship and caution is a delicate one that needs constant monitoring.

Reinventing the Wheel

The time and effort required to implement business and industry programs is phenomenal. It may take a number of staff members six to ten meetings to analyze, develop, and sell the program. Where degree programs are repetitious, training is normally a once-and-done course. The tremendous effort that was expended to develop and deliver the program can never be used again.

To avoid reinventing the wheel with each new CJT contract, college staff can use previous programs as models for new ones. But, each and every effective CJT program is as the name applies—customized. Companies want training that meets their specific needs, and, thus, the program inevitably must be unique.

Another seemingly inevitable problem that develops with CJT programming is the short lead time requested by most businesses. While degree programs are carefully planned well in advance, CJT programs may have to be developed under very accelerated schedules. Major firms are often very bureaucratic and slow to make decisions, but once a training proposal is accepted, the firm wants the training to begin immediately. The college needs to be realistic in what it can accomplish and must protect itself in the contracting process while still giving the firm the best service possible.

Evaluation

Evaluation has a multifaceted application for both traditional and CJT programs. Both can utilize a pretest for entrance. However, any industry pretest, by federal regulations, must be proved to be job related to avoid any chance of bias or discrimination. As such, all CJT pretests must be cross-referenced to job competencies to prove the validity of each question in determining entrance requirements. This strict procedure is not mandated for degree programs.

While traditional programs are evaluated on criteria such as whether students are attracted to the program, the quality of the faculty and facilities, whether students get jobs, and how well they do in those jobs after graduation, CJT programs are evaluated on the increased job performance of trainees as a direct result of the training, whether there is a reduction in down time, and whether there is a decrease in the amount of waste.

Promotional Strategy

Training programs must have an entirely different promotional strategy from traditional programs. Ongoing programs focus on the eighteen- to twenty-year-old recent high school graduate. For CJT programs, the target population to contact, interest, and convince consists of the critical corporate personnel who make corporate training decisions.

One-on-one contact is the best approach. Breakfast meetings with the chief executive officer (CEO) can develop an ally for the college at the top of the company. Once a firm's CEO is convinced of the benefits of college based training, the selling process is much easier.

News releases and trade articles also need to be a part of each college's promotional plan, and success stories about CJT programs are important tools for the dissemination of information.

The key to successful promotion of CJT is to know your target population, arrange a personal one-on-one visit, and sell the program. Once the successes start, word-of-mouth referrals and repeat business will ensure program continuation and expansion.

Involvement with the Client

In traditional degree programs, the college has a two-year involvement with a student that, unfortunately, can be rather transitory. CJT programs create the possibility of a continuing involvement of the college with each company it serves. The delivery of quality training programs that satisfy company needs will ensure the company's return for additional programs. The repetitive nature of training means that the college need add only four or five new companies a year while concentrating its efforts on repeat business. Systematic follow-up with each company is obviously critical.

Technological Innovation

CJT, especially when funded by state or federal grants, allows for a degree of technical innovation that does not exist in ongoing courses and programs. Examples include the development of training manuals for the specific operations of a company; the development of a full range of audiovisual materials for a specific program; and the ability to choose state-of-the-art faculty without having to retrain current staff. The involvement with industry will give community college educators a different perspective on training.

Labor Relations

No training program can be a success at a unionized company without union support. Care must be taken at each step to assure the union representatives that the program is a fair one and that it has been designed based on input from labor and management. It is also important that any pretests are identifiably job related and that remedial instruction is available for those who do not pass the first pretest.

The key to working with unions is to show them clearly the long-term benefits for their employees. For example, in some cases a training program may increase a company's profitability and thus prevent layoffs. While the firm's management can best handle almost all union contact, institutional personnel may need to explain the program to the union leaders.

Conclusion

Education and training are both integral components of the comprehensive community college. The idiosyncrasies of the two types of offerings must be considered when an institution either enters the industrial training mode of operation or expands its efforts in this area. Effective administrators must be aware of the similarities and differences between education and industrial training, and they must plan carefully to minimize the impact of training programs on the institution's total mission.

References

Averill, D. F., "The Mission of Vocational Education and Trends in Training Delivery." In *Collaboration: Vocational Education and the Private Secotr — 1984 Yearbook of the American Vocational Association.* Arlington, Va.: American Vocational Association, 1984.

Goldman, S. L., and Sutcliffe, S. H. "STS, Technology Literacy, and Arts Curriculum." *Bull. Sci. Tech. Soc.,* 1982, 2, 291–307.

Peters, T. J., and Waterman, R. H., Jr. *In Search of Excellence.* New York: Harper & Row, 1982.

Warmbrod, C. P., and Faddis, C. R. *Retraining and Upgrading Workers: A Guide for Postsecondary Educators.* Columbus: Ohio State University, National Center for Research in Vocational Education, 1983.

Webster's New Collegiate Dictionary, (2nd ed.) 1977.

Robert G. Clarke is president of Vermont Technical College, Randolph Center, Vermont.

The centralized organizational model offers the greatest chances of success for colleges responding to business and industry's training needs.

Providing Customized Job Training Through the Traditional Administrative Organizational Model

William A. Connor

The selection and utilization of community and junior colleges as providers of training and educational services to business and industry is of benchmark significance in the continuum of growth, development, and achievement for the two-year college movement. There is little doubt now that the introduction of industrial training into the two-year college environment will represent one third of the most historical events in all of higher education for the decade of the eighties. Those who have been a part of or close to the two-year college boom since the mid sixties will understand the impact of this event. It would have been impossible at that time, given the business and economic climate, the prevailing management and organizational practices, and the general understanding and acceptance of two-year colleges by the corporate world, for this most appropriate marriage to have occurred.

At stake, then, in the two-year college system's response to this opportunity is the complete integration of the two-year college system

R. Kopecek, R. Clarke (Eds.). *Customized Job Training for Business and Industry.*
New Directions for Community Colleges, no. 48. San Francisco: Jossey-Bass, December 1984.

into the mainstream of all of higher education as a unique but different type of institution, whose outcomes are equal in societal and economic benefit to any other segment. Surely, the system would have achieved this stature eventually through many different modes, but it can do so now by demonstrating training and educational results that improve life quality for participants, that help them actualize their social and economic pursuits, that meet business and industry expectations, and that achieve the bottom line — the economic growth and development of the country.

For the past sixty years, Americans have viewed our great universities as the citadels of professional schools and research centers, our fine colleges as the home of the liberal arts and of career preparation. How has the two-year college been viewed during this period? As the "junior" element in the educational process; as the "second-chance" institution; as the "experimenting," "finding one's self" opportunity; as the first two years of an education to be finished somewhere else? Whatever or however it has been regarded, it is clear now by the footpaths of students, by the decisions in the corporate board rooms, and by the actions of local, state, and national government, that a part of the two-year college system is seen distinctively as a technical training resource, serving individuals and firms as an "area developer" (according to some chambers of commerce), producing discernible economic development advantages at a cost-benefit ratio unparalleled in American higher education history.

Historically, educators have believed that organization is a key to successful goal attainment. So firmly has this thought been ingrained, that eons of time have been spent devising, testing, and writing about management organization. Educators have analyzed, overanalyzed, and superanalyzed organizational patterns, fine-tuning them every few years or sooner, hoping to make their institutions able to respond more effectively to student and community needs. More organizational charts have been drawn in the last thirty years than significant works of art. In all of this quest for organizational utopia, I am reminded of the simple words of Freud who once said "and no matter what amount of analyzing, studying, and theories evolve about the cigar — it's simply a cigar" Freud, 1960, p. 123). Perhaps that is where we really stand with management and organization.

Why is management organization of any importance to customized job training (CJT)? Clearly, many colleges want to position their internal and external resources in such a manner as to maximize their opportunity to succeed. The quest for this maximization leads to the manipulation of the college's current organization or to experimentation with new forms as a way of contributing to effectiveness.

The Centralized Organizational Model

For the purpose of this chapter, the centralized or traditional two-year college organizational model for the delivery of training and/or educational services to specific groups and organizations, including business and industry, is featured. Again, however, it must be stressed that the model is not presented as the universal ideal. There is no one correct or incorrect organizational service delivery model. What is correct is a model, with all the necessary localized modifications, that works for the given situation.

The centralized, traditional model is one that holds a single office responsible for the entrepreneuring, planning, coordinating, organizing, and, in many instances, operating and evaluating of all continuing education, customized job training, and unique educational courses or programs of a credit or credit-free nature, on or off campus, that are conducted for discrete populations. These populations might consist of current employees of the business and industrial complex, potential employees in pre-employment training or preparation conducted by companies at their expense, unemployed individuals in a variety of special programs, CETA/PIC (Comprehensive Educational Training Act/Private Industry Council) clients, and employees of social service, health, and recreational organizations within the community.

This model is characterized by the presence of a key administrative staff person leading the single office at the dean or director level, depending on institutional size, with necessary support staff in numbers related to the volume of work produced. This lead individual tends to be regarded as an academic generalist.

The obvious strengths of this model are its control and accountability features. Control in this instance is referred to in a management rather than a psychological sense. Key information in and out of the institution, critical decisions (including the curriculum design and presentation), along with all the other related support requirements for specialized courses and programs, are funneled through one office and ultimately one administrator.

At the same time, this model also has an obvious weakness — the need for strong coordination with other offices and support centers on the campus.

Examining the scope of activities of a typical centralized continuing education office (listed in the next section), some educators argue that all the responsibilities required for an educationally sound program can be handled adequately except perhaps for one — but that one is the central one — the planning, designing, organizing, and presenting of a unified, customized curriculum aimed specifically at the precise needs of the external group. It is true that no single administrator has the discipline range to handle this key responsibility adequately—nor should she or he be expected to. Thus, in the centralized model, there is the need to involve and coordinate with the discipline "expert" on campus or off who holds the technical expertise necessary to produce a quality curriculum. I submit that an academic generalist, with background and experience in curriculum development, can adequately coordinate any curriculum requirements.

Even with this limitation, the model holds distinct advantages over the totally decentralized model in that almost all business and industrial organizations large enough to support their own training staff have organized themselves under the centralized model. Therefore, when they approach a college with adjunct training or educational needs, they find it easier to deal with a familiar organizational structure.

Needs and Responsibilities of the Centralized Office

Setting aside, for a moment, the key curriculum design and faculty resource needs of each specialized program, we can examine a fairly typical listing of understandings, skills, and abilities that the centralized office needs to possess in planning routine courses or programs:

- The need to know the community well (The key administrator of the centralized office must be active in a broad range of community activities.)
- A thorough knowledge of the history and current operation of the college
- A working acquaintanceship with community college law, rules and regulations, sponsorship agreements, funding, full-time enrollment (FTE) requirements, and so on
- The ability to prepare accurate course and/or program budgets and to develop pricing practices
- Planning skills, including strong one-on-one communication strengths and group management expertise
- The ability to prepare descriptive promotional materials and to develop an advertising plan and budget
- Flexible standard setting with regard to time, place, and class scheduling
- Registration and student accounting (record-keeping) requirements
- Tuition and fee payment plans including financial aid as necessary
- Health requirements, if any

- Counseling, advising, and placement services
- Insurance requirements, if appropriate
- Curriculum planning and scheduling
- Textbook procurement along with the selection and purchase of any related consumable supplies or capital instructional or noninstructional equipment
- Faculty selection, appointment, payment, and evaluation
- Maintenance of all appropriate college entrance requirements as well as all other related academic or nonacademic policies
- Classroom selection and reservation
- Grant applications, as appropriate
- Letter writing and general communication requirements
- Supervision and emergency procedures
- Course or program evaluation and information dissemination
- The ability to elicit cooperation and cordial working relationships with other college offices.

An analysis of this fairly typical scope of responsibilities immediately exposes the major weakness of the decentralized model: Often these functions are repeated by a number of college staff for offerings native to specific departments or divisions, thereby introducing a time and function inefficiency into the system. When it is realized that time is finite and is expended in direct relationship to outcomes and income, colleges will be far more sensitive about managing their time-outcome ratios.

At the same time, however, many colleges of 1,500 FTEs or more have found this list of responsibilities too extensive for a single office to manage. Therefore, it is not atypical for certain activities, native to all customized or external educational programs, to be separated from the central office and assigned to one or more competent support offices. These activities tend to include advertising, registration, recordkeeping, counseling, advising, placement, financial aid, tuition payments, and health and insurance requirements.

Conversely, some colleges, deeply committed to the centralized model, insist on the total turnkey arrangement regardless of their size.

The reason these differing approaches exist is the fact that some colleges see many of elements of CJT as "noninstructional" and thereby manageable by noninstructional staff. Other institutions see all the elements as instructionally related and insist on academic control. The latter institutions tend to be those strongly committed to the centralized model.

If the weight of the instructionally related requirements listed here is insufficient to convince the reader of the control advantages and time efficiencies of the centralized model, then turning attention to the direct instructional requirements of the office will bring us to the margin of difference between the two most popular organizational modes in use today.

Company-College Relationships and Centralized Organization

In most business and industrial firms of 500 or more employees, a training office with its attendant support staff is in place. This office organizes generic training programs within the firm by consulting with appropriate management and mid-management personnel in its various departments. The in-house training personnel are not seen as experts in all the potential instructional fields the company may require to meet its employees and its own growth needs. Rather, they are seen as competent generalists who know how to conceptualize and plan an effective educational experience after hearing problem statements and outcome objectives. Teaching resources are then drawn from the company itself or secured externally from business consultants, commercial training firms, or from the faculty of colleges and universities.

This system is not puzzling to the company training officer. It is not only typical of the field but it is also expected, since it seems—for business and industry anyway—to contribute to an efficient time-outcome ratio. Top company managers simply do not want key unit leadership, mid-management personnel, or product specialists serving as training planners or organizers. They are being paid, not as educators, but as individuals whose primary attention is on marketing, planning, designing, managing, communicating, production, quality control, sales, traffic, and profits.

When a company approaches a college or a service deliverer for programs, courses, or training experiences that it cannot readily provide itself, it does so from the experience and action base just described. Finding a centralized college-based response model in place is likely to engender an immediate confidence level in company officials, since they perceive that the college operates similarly to their own current practice. Such a model is likely to lead to a satisfactory result, provided the representatives of the college and of the company see themselves as a team responsible for program planning.

In the decentralized model (no matter how decentralized), it is desirable for an external contact to have a "point-of-entry" relationship with some "one" individual from the college. Should this individual be a curriculum content person or a generalist? Remember that the decentralizationists claim that their goal is to match the appropriate institutional curriculum content expert in a given field with a specialist in business or industry who knows intimately the "customs" that need to be taught. If the primary match is made between a college content specialist and a company specialist, both must involve additional parties in order to manage all the instruction-related program requirements. This scenario, in effect, is a transposed or inverted centralized model, but it now involves a team of at least four.

If the primary match is made between a college content specialist and a company generalist, a planning mismatch occurs and each side ends up confused. Hopefully, each is wise enough to recognize what is occurring and take corrective action. The history of college content specialists working with company generalists has not been a glowing one. Companies tend to feel that their program was not "customized" but rather that it was "standardized" (Scharlatt, 1983, p. 42).

Finally, if the point-of-entry contact is made between a college generalist and company generalist, we have, in effect, the centralized model at work, no matter what the institution's organizational pattern may suggest or the chief executive officer may think.

However, most colleges utilizing the decentralized approach are hoping to match the company's point-of-entry person, whomever it might be, with a highly competent content specialist whose role is likely to be to "talk tech."

The company representative may well be impressed with this commitment to specialization, and, in fact, it might work well. However, the college's point-of-entry person, if a content specialist, will not likely end up providing or even knowing of all the instruction-related requirements for a quality program, thus forcing the college to add an additional person or to involve a combination of offices to provide for those ancillary needs with, of course, their attendant campuswide communication and coordination risks.

One remaining point must be made on college-company relationships before moving on to another concept. The previous paragraphs have assumed that companies were of sufficient size to have their own training departments. Let us consider for a moment the myriad of business organizations too small to have such an office. The Department of Labor has predicted that by the year 2000, 85 percent of all companies will be in the "small business" category with less than 500 employees. This category, incidentally, showed the largest current national training budget increase in 1983 (Zemke, Budgets. . . ," 1983). How are these companies organizing themselves today for training purposes? The current model is for a high-ranking management officer or for the person handling personnel and contract functions to manage the external training effort. Matching a college content specialist with a company executive or a personnel type is likely to be a mismatch. This leaves the institution with the question of who shall relate to a company generalist — an academic generalist or a content specialist? The former may have the skills to state the training problems and identify and confirm what is needed, while the latter may provide too heavy an academic view, being unable to separate degree-level education from company training needs.

Looking at the issue from prior two-year college practice further supports the centralized model. Hardly any institution from the community college sector has deviated from the central vice-president-for-academic-affairs or dean-of-instruction mode of organization with respect to academic administration. These position holders, while grounded in at least one academic discipline, fill the role of the academic generalist for the entire institution. We have almost been religious in our insistence on maintaining the control and accountability features of centralized academic leadership for the college, but we seem to be willing to experiment with the use of the decentralized model to serve such an important new and potentially mission-changing client market as the training and retraining needs of the American business and industrial complex.

The time-proven aspects of the centralized model, as illustrated at any institutional and organizational level where it is utilized, are its strong planning, control, and accountability features. While it might be argued that more external service can be provided through a cadre of academic entrepreneurs operating like a sales force throughout a college's service area, it is likely that the apparent immediate numerical success of this method could lead to a decline in repeat service if the features of centralization are not ensured. Most educators have learned that there is no quick, overnight, Federal Express or telephone marketing for quality instruction; however, the field continues to attract new professionals who must learn this truth only after the experience of unfulfilled goals.

At the same time, it is odd that representatives of business and industry — especially those who have had the experience of planning and operating in-house or plant-focused educational programs — would themselves not be skeptical of the decentralized, quickly established educational experience. Business and industrial trainers have tended to report that such an approach has not worked for them (Smith, 1982).

Although business and industry are approaching the two-year college for important training needs, some are doing so with caution or with, at best, a "let's try one program and see" approach. Why jeopardize this potential major new educational relationship by responding with an administrative organizational structure that is atypical in terms of history and practice and one that has as its weakness a communication and coordination element that places almost all the potential for breakdown on the college side? In fact, the major strength of the decentralized model—speed providing direct instructional service—is the very feature that tends to activate its major weakness. In other words, the faster the service that is committed by a college staff person (who is not required to plan and conduct all related program or course requirements), the greater the strain on the communication, coordination, and delivery essentials that other staff must provide to ensure a quality educational experience, and the greater the threat to company satisfaction.

Organizational Structure and Program Evaluation

It has been stated tenfold and a hundred that no well-conceived educational experience ends without an effectively designed evaluation instrument. In the decentralized model, who is responsible for program or course evaluation? Is it the content specialist who, in all likelihood, had a role in content preparation, the outcome objectives, and the recommendation for faculty employment? How might this individual, who was so closely involved in the program itself, view the evaluation process? Should the evaluation be conducted by a campus generalist? Is an individual who provided some or all of the instruction-related requirements a likely candidate, or should a supergeneralist having little direct contact with the program draw this assignment? If these questions are even pondered on the college campus, then it would appear that organizational structure is an issue that needs resolution.

The question of who shall evaluate is really a question of who is in charge or, better yet, of who is accountable. There are no such dichotomous questions when it comes to who is responsible for evaluating campus-based degree programs or certificate instruction. It is the chief academic officer who traditionally and rightfully meets this requirement.

The accountability issue is perhaps the key element to consider when weighing the pros and cons of the use of a centralized or decentralized administrative organizational model to respond to external service needs. Viewing the evaluation requirement in isolation from all the other instruction-related requirements should point up its critical importance in confirming program strengths and in identifying weaknesses that require action. The institution's response to the weaknesses represents the single most crucial element in the process—the need to identify honestly program areas requiring redress and then take those actions decisively that bolster external confidence and connote to the external markets that the institution will not replicate a less-than-quality experience. These kinds of administrative behaviors will surely tend to build confidence, solidify the relationship, and engender repeat contacts with the external organization.

The opposite is almost predictable in the institution that has not clearly identified a single responsible office to be held accountable for *all* customized job training. In an organizational structure that has become so decentralized that accountability is vague, the office that draws the assignment to evaluate program outcomes is the very one that is likely to be the least objective.

Conclusion

In this chapter, the appropriateness of the traditional administrative organizational model as a response mechanism to requests from business and industry for training and educational services has been presented. The critical need for effective results, so that the town-and-gown cooperation in economic development—only in its infancy stage—reaches full maturity to the benefit of industry, colleges, and society, has been stressed.

The arguments and the rationale for the traditional model have been drawn almost purely from the academic perspective. As a reinforcement to the position developed in this chapter, the view of business and industry can serve as an appropriate conclusion.

In a 1981 study of forty-eight of California's largest corporations, conducted by Curtis R. Hungerford, professor of educational administration at Brigham Young University, industry leadership identified five problems they perceive in developing cooperative training and education programs with higher education (Schleyer, 1982). Hungerford reported that one of the five was that industry training leaders "apparently distrust academic types" (p. 28). Industry trainers matched with high academicians for curricular content discussions were left with the impression that the educational institution could not meet industry's "real-world" needs. What a shame that industry was given a view of academic perspective, environment, and response that is not typical. Once again it appears clear that if business and industry are going to approach colleges and universities with generally but broadly prepared training officers, personnel managers, or senior management types, the colleges side, if it wants to serve effectively, must respond with its best academic generalists who are well founded in curriculum planning, design, and organization and who, at the same time, have a strong pragmatic view of the marketplace, the community, and society at large.

References

Freud, E. L. (Ed.) *Letters of Sigmund Freud.* New York: Basic Books, 1960.

Scharlatt, H. "Customized Training: Great Work If You Can Get It." *Training: The Magazine of Human Resource Development,* August 1983, p. 42–44.

Schleyer, R. J. "Why Can't Business and Education Get Together?" *Training: The Magazine of Human Resource Development,* March 1982, p. 28.

Smith, J. "A Trainer's Guide to Successful Productivity Improvement Planning." *Training: The Magazine of Human Resource Development,* March 1982, p. 41–44.

Zemke, R. "Training Budgets '83: A Case of the Blahs." *Training: The Magazine of Human Resource Development,* October 1983, p. 34–39.

William A. Connor is president of Sussex County Community College in New Jersey.

A unique approach to customized training which takes into
account issues related to traditional labor-management
problems, the need to reflect a broad-based and grassroots
involvement of targeted groups, and the need to base the
training method and content upon identified, job-related
competencies is described.

Developing Customized Programs for Steel and Other Heavy Industries

Philip R. Day, Jr.

The "Put America Back to Work" project sponsored by the American Association of Community and Junior Colleges (AACJC) emphasizes the need for a concerted national effort to ensure that a well-trained work force is available to operate the businesses and industries of the future. Without this effort, the road to a healthier, more productive, competitive, and technologically up-to-date private sector will be far more difficult (Ellison and others, 1983). The nation's 1,234 community and technical colleges are the cornerstone of this emerging economic and human resource development stragety. Located within easy commuting distance of most individuals in the United States, they represent a tremendous capital investment, and they are now providing high-quality, modestly priced, custom-designed training for American businesses and industry. Because of the magnitude of the problems, however, more needs to be done to reduce the widening schism between the "haves" and "have nots," to put America back to work, and to assist the country in maintaining its traditional industrial and manufacturing leadership.

R. Kopecek, R. Clarke (Eds.). *Customized Job Training for Business and Industry.*
New Directions for Community Colleges, no. 48. San Francisco: Jossey-Bass, December 1984.

Dundalk Community College, located in the southeastern corner of Baltimore County, is situated, like other such institutions, within a heavily industrialized sector of our country. The college operates its programs and services in the shadows of such giants as General Motors, Western Electric, Bethlehem Steel shipyard, and the largest employer of them all, Bethlehem Steel (Sparrows Point plant). Unlike most community colleges who have attempted to offer a range of services and training programs to support both the training needs of the "working adults" and the large employers and have been frustrated or discouraged in their efforts, Dundalk has been successful in implementing a unique approach to customized training. The approach takes into account issues related to traditional labor-management problems, the need to reflect a broad-based and grass-roots involvement of targeted groups, and the need to base the training method and content upon identified, job-related competencies, thereby ensuring its success.

Training Issues

Carnavale and Goldstin (1983) in their book, *Employee Training: Its Changing Role and Analysis of New Data,* illustrate underinvestment in human resources, particularly in the current work force. Twenty-six percent of American working adults are functionally illiterate. Nearly 6 percent of the civilian work force suffers from alcoholism, costing the economy more than $28 billion a year in lost production. A large number of workers who possess clerical or technological skills are retiring and replacements are not being trained. The annual turnover rate in the manufacturing labor force involves one-third of all workers, significantly reducing productivity. Public incentives favor overwhelmingly capital and technological investments over worker training as a way to improve productivity. In reality, this phenomenon reflects the need of the industries to upgrade their capital equipment inventories and to bring on high-technology and automated manufacturing systems in an attempt to keep pace with the world markets. However, the problems associated with the industry's current inability to keep up with these changes, particularly those related to providing timely and relevant training opportunities to the current work force, further complicate some of the problems that we in two-year college education are going to have to be aware of and, more importantly, develop strategies to accommodate.

Dundalk's Service Region — Problems and Outlook

All of these problems have had an impact on Dundalk Community College's service region. The area has been hit by inordinately high rates of unemployment. While state and regional figures continue to ease down slightly from the all-time high of over 10 percent, the figures of the greater Dundalk service region hover between 22 and 25 percent. This situation is in large measure due to the decline in employment potential at three of the major industrial facilities: General Motors, the Bethlehem Steel plant (Sparrows Point), and the Bethlehem Steel shipyard. Total employment for these firms has gone from a level in 1978 of 29,039 to 16,689 in 1982 (Hoffman and Schwartz, 1982).

For the steel industry, developments locally are merely a reflection of what has happened on a national level. Steel production in the United States has been declining since 1974. From 1975 to 1980, capacity utilization remained at about 80 percent before plunging in 1981 and 1982. Similarly, total employment in the steel industry nationally dropped from about 500,000 in 1974 to 400,000 in 1980 and 1981, and it declined sharply in the first half of 1982 to just over 300,000 (Iron and Steel Institute, 1982).

Steel economists and industry spokespersons expect that the 1982 recession will cause eight to seventeen million tons of industrial capacity to disappear, representing about six plants and 50,000 jobs. Some of the capacity can be made up by upgrading other plants, but the jobs are a permanent loss to the industry (Chavez, 1982). In the spring of 1982, 50 percent of capacity was the average for the American steel industry and for the Sparrows Point plant. By June 1982, the industry slashed production to only 43 percent of capacity, the lowest level since the second Roosevelt administration, and 106,000 workers were on layoffs and another 28,000 were working short weeks. Production dropped further to 40 percent by September 1982. Sparrows Point continues to equal the national average (Hoffman and Schwartz, 1982).

On July 30, 1981, Bethlehem Steel's chairman, Donald H. Trautlein, announced plans calling for a $750 million investment and modernization program. About half of this sum will be spent at Sparrows Point (Trautlein, 1981). Modernization of the plate mills at the Sparrows Point plant was one of three projects to begin immediately, and engineering was announced as underway on installation of a continuous slab caster and on modernization of the sixty-eight-inch hot-strip mill, both at Sparrows Point. In addition, Mr. Trautlein noted that Bethlehem Steel was nearing completion of a $170 million coke oven battery at Sparrows Point. The Sparrows Point $225 million "L" blast furnace began operation in 1978, and it is the largest iron-making facility in the Western Hemisphere. It is an automated facility that daily exceeds its rated capacity of 8,000 tons of iron.

It is important to understand that even with the future modernization and investment plans targeted for Sparrows Point, the expected recovery will not mean that the employment outlook for the plant will ever approximate previous levels. Hoffman and Schwartz (1982) forecast both a high and a low employment outlook for the Sparrows Point plant as well as other major industries. At best, the total employment level is not expected to be in excess of 10,000. The worst-case scenario calls for an employment level at or near 5,000.

Sparrows Point's Operational Maintenance Initiative

The Maintenance Management System that Sparrows Point worked with from 1973 to 1984 proved to be very beneficial in mills where everyone made a good effort to use it. Even in areas where it was only partially used, it provided some degree of benefit. This system did not answer all needs completely, but it did point out that the maintenance labor force was not being fully utilized and was not flexible enough. Still, even with good participation by operating and maintenance supervisors, the system's inflexibility could not generate enough forces for good repair turnaround. The levels of supervision employed at the time insulated middle and top management from the hourly forces and did not utilize the best creative resources of the hourly ranks (Bethlehem Steel, 1982).

The system allowed only a few of the hourly personnel to participate in the maintenance planning effort and, in fact, discouraged the ideas of hourly people. Communications among the different layers of management personnel clearly demonstrated that, except in a few cases, the hourly ranks had only physical input to the maintenance effort. Since hourly workers did not feel they were a real part of the effort, they lacked commitment to the system.

The Bethlehem firm has made a strong commitment to adapt to a new concept of maintenance. The concept evolved from a series of visits to Japanese steel plants — Nippon Steel, Nippon Kokan, and Sumitomo Metal — all of which had in place an operational maintenance program noted for its efficiency and direct hourly worker participation. This style of maintenance is new to the American steel industry, but it has been employed in Japan, and a similar system has been used in Europe, for ten years. When the plan was first introduced to the maintenance departments at Sparrows Point, there were many concerns about how to structure the work force and get operator involvement in the design and implementation of the concept (Bethlehem Steel, 1982).

The fact that many of the hourly employees were fearful of additional job losses and were generally suspicious about any new proposals offered by management did not make for an easy beginning. However, the company made a major commitment to involve hourly, salaried, and supervisory personnel who were potentially impacted by this new concept on several planning committees and task forces responsible for developing the overall implementation strategies for the "Point." One of the main concerns of the operators (that is, the hourly personnel) was the part of the concept that gives the operator the control of all operating support functions that are not related to the repair effort; under the "old" maintenance effort, these functions were performed by other personnel. Everyone recognized that the transfer of these functions would require a great deal of input and cooperation among all parties.

One very important part of the operational maintenance plan was to provide technical training to maintenance personnel and operators, as needed, to ensure that work can be done well. A key person in this maintenance concept would be the hourly inspector-planner coordinator. This person would inspect, plan repairs, procure necessary parts and tools, schedule the work, request the necessary manpower, and monitor the repairs on returns. Obviously, the person would have to be well trained in order for the system to work. This position was to have a new classification for Bethlehem and, as such, individuals would have to be selected from the current work force and "retrained" to fulfill the position's responsibilities. Estimates on the total number of positions varied, but the range fell between 200 and 350 personnel.

Dundalk Community College's Response

Dundalk Community College and Bethlehem Steel had previously worked on several less elaborate programs leading to an arts associate (A.A.) degree in millwright technology and electrical technology. Previous programs had always involved voluntary training and skill upgrading on the part of the Bethlehem employees. Program and curriculum development efforts essentially followed traditional paths and were a result of efforts of individual faculty operating in isolation with some level of input from advisory committees or using the survey-interview approach that has been the cornerstone of most programmatic development efforts in career training.

Since the new training program was characterized by full-time required involvement, coupled with general fear and anxiety and a lack of trust on the part of potential participants, a tailored process was suggested by college officials as the method for developing the program. If the program was to succeed, emphasis needed to be placed on analyzing projected and specific functions and competencies associated with this new position, getting direct grass-roots involvement in the process, and finally, getting concurrence from both hourly and salaried personnel, management, and the union — not an easy task.

The *DACUM: Identifying Competencies* (Miller-Beach, 1980) model of curriculum development was chosen. I had utilized the process with considerable success in other institutions and was knowledgeable of the success that others had with the model. To date, over 400 curriculum programs have been developed utilizing this approach. I felt that the model was well suited for application in this case.

The DACUM Customized Approach

For developers of competency-based instructional programs, DACUM (Developing a Curriculum) is a relatively quick and inexpensive method for determining which competencies should be included in a curriculum. Created and first used by the Experimental Projects Branch, Canada Department of Regional Economic Expansion, and the General Learning Corporation of New York, DACUM is based on three assumptions: (1) Expert workers can define and describe their jobs more accurately than anyone else; (2) any job can be effectively described in terms of the tasks that successful workers in that occupation perform; and (3) all tasks, in order to be performed correctly, demand certain knowledge and attitudes from workers.

The process requires a panel of expert workers and supervisors from the occupation being analyzed, a qualified facilitator in Dundalk's case (Jack Harris, director of staff and program development, Stark Technical College, Canton, Ohio), and a recorder. In three days the panel develops a profile chart of the skills required in the occupation. A DACUM chart serves both as a curriculum plan and as an instrument for assesing training needs and student achievement (Adams, 1975).

The five-step process (Miller-Beach, 1980) is outlined here:

1. Panel members identify the general areas of competency required.

2. Focusing on only one area at a time, the panel specifies the skills required in each of the categories. Each skill statement is recorded on a card and posted beside the appropriate category. Eventually, the category statement, together with the skill statement, form a "competency band" on the chart. It is imperative that each statement contain precise action terms, such as "detect and diagnose engine faults."

3. After the skills required in each category have been identified, panelists make sure that each skill statement is explicit and accurate.

4. Skill statements are structured into a learning sequence.

Panelists decide which skills an entry-level worker should learn and apply first on the job. The statements are then arranged in order.

5. The facilitator solicits the panelists' consensus regarding the accuracy of the chart. They should agree that it correctly reflects the skills required in that occupation.

In the DACUM workshop conducted for Bethlehem Steel, since the position was a "new job," we selected panelists who had at least some experience with the different aspects of this new position. Fourteen hourly employes and first-line supervisors spent two days at the college identifying the competencies needed for the Inspector-Planner Program. The facilitator's role was to hammer out the final competency-based chart.

Historically, the relations between steel unions and management have not been good. Consequently, there was a healthy dose of mutual distrust at the beginning of the process. Gradually this distrust was replaced with an esprit de corps brought about by the shared goal and the consensus building inherent to DACUM. At the end of the two-day period, the group had identified 126 different competencies for the Inspector-Planner Program.

Utilization of the DACUM process ensured that all of the training would be job related because now the college had a clear means of documenting the origin of the training program. A concomitant benefit was the positive attitude that developed on the part of the hourly employees and the first-line supervisors who had participated in this new training program.

While the DACUM group was meeting, several faculty and Bethlehem Steel staff members met to get acquainted with the broad objectives of the program. Additionally, in-service training was conducted to help faculty and "Point" personnel understand the competency-based approach and the integration of identified competencies into curriculum development efforts. This effort was directed by Curtis Miles, dean of education resource development, Piedmont Technical College, South Carolina. Once objectives were identified, the DACUM panel members and the curriculum development group met to make sure that the faculty understood the competencies that had been identified (see Figure 1 for a selected listing). Using these competencies, the faculty, "Point" people, and selected members of the panel developed a thirty-week, full-time curriculum that was job related.

With these competencies as a basis for the curriculum development effort, both the faculty and the company employees found this to be a challenging and rewarding process, since both groups had to test their ideas in an unfamiliar atmosphere. The faculty was intrigued with the opportunity to take educational theory and apply it to a real-

Figure 1. DACUM Matrix of Occupational Competencies — Dundalk Community College

INSPECTOR-PLANNER

A. PRACTICE SAFETY	1. Follow company safety program	2. Follow OSHA, MOSHA, Federal and state regulations	3. Use emergency numbers and calling procedures	4. Select and use appropriate fire extinguishers	5. Select and use appropriate safety equipment i.e., personal equipment, stretchers, etc.	6. Use specialized tools i.e., spark-proof, insulated	7. Read Job Safety Analyses	8. Use signs and warning devices
	9. Demonstrates basic first aid techniques	10. Demonstrate confined space procedures	11. Demonstrate proper rigging, lifting and control techniques	12. Demonstrate shut-down and start-up procedures	13. Demonstrate proper use of portable equipment i.e., lighting, ventilation, pumping	14. Demonstrate proper use of platforms and scaffolding	15. Demonstrate good housekeeping procedures	16. Follow heat alert procedures (and hypothermia)
B. DEMONSTRATE KNOWLEDGE OF HAZARDOUS MATERIALS AND CONDITIONS	1. Demonstrate knowledge of gas properties	2. Demonstrate knowledge of atmospheric test equipment	3. Demonstrate knowledge of hazards and properties of chemicals	4. Demonstrate knowledge of hazards and properties of materials	5. Demonstrate awareness of special hazards i.e., radiation, PCB's	6. Follow safe hazardous waste disposal		
C. DEMONSTRATE JOB PROFICIENCY	Demonstrate basic understanding of:	(Electrical and Mechanical)	1. bearings	2. burning and welding	3. alignment	4. basic metallurgy	5. gearing	6. fits and clearance
	7. layout and fabrication	8. hydraulics and pneumatics	9. electrical/electronic fundamentals	10. physics and mechanical principles	11. rigging principles	12. pumps and cylinders	13. instrumentation	14. refrigeration and air conditioning
	15. steam and pressure	16. turbines, blowers, and fans	17. thermodynamics	18. mechanical/electrical interlocking sequence	19. adhesives and sealants	20. fasteners	21. conveyor systems	22. wirerope, and reeving
	23. drives and transmissions	24. tools	25. power transmission couplings	26. hoses	27. seals and packing	28. wear-resistant and protective liners (tanks, bins, and chutes)	(Mechanical)	29. pipe fitting and tubing
	(Electrical)	30. AC/DC motor theory and generators	31. transformer theory	32. conductors, insulators and conduit	33. electrical regulators	34. high voltage switch gear	35. principles of batteries	

D. DEMONSTRATE COMMUNICATION ABILITY	1. Demonstrate ability to communicate technical information	2. Demonstrate ability to communicate with other departments effectively	3. Demonstrate interpersonal relationships	4. Demonstrate knowledge of organizational and departmental duties	5. Demonstrate basic writing skills	6. Demonstrate leadership abilities	7. Demonstrate positive reinforcement abilities	8. Demonstrate patience
	9. Demonstrate ability to follow instructions	10. Demonstrate ability to listen	11. Demonstrate ability to solicit input					
E. DEMONSTRATE UNDERSTANDING OF INSPECTION TECHNIQUES AND PLANNING	1. Establish inspection routes and frequencies	2. Establish preventive maintenance routes and frequencies	3. Establish inspection procedures	4. Demonstrate diagnostic procedures	5. Establish and maintain equipment histories	6. Demonstrate basic understanding of planning techniques	7. Write job requests	8. Schedule work
	9. Demonstrate basic understanding of sequencing work	10. Demonstrate basic understanding of cost effectiveness	11. Utilize all resources	12. Process appropriate paper work	13. Use date processing	14. Demonstrate basic typing		
F. USE PARTS SYSTEM	1. Demonstrate basic understanding of supply process	2. Establish and maintain critical parts list	3. Utilize CRT	4. Identify parts needed	5. Confirm parts availability	6. Order necessary parts	7. Receive and inspect parts	8. Arrange for removal of parts
	9. Arrange for rebuilding parts	10. Arrange for modifying parts	11. Return unused parts to inventory	12. Report part usage to inventory control				
G. READ AND INTERPRET ENGINEERING DRAWINGS	1. Demonstrate ability to sketch	2. Read and interpret schematics	3. Read and interpret blueprints	4. Read and interpret exploded diagrams	5. Read and interpret catalogs and technical manuals	6. Arrange for update and changing of engineering drawings		
H. USE TESTING AND MEASURING DEVICES	1. Identify equipment available	2. Keep abreast of state of the art equipment	3. Demonstrate ability to use electrical testing measuring devices	4. Demonstrate use of size measuring equipment	5. Demonstrate use of vibration test equipment	6. Demonstrate use of temperature test equipment	7. Demonstrate use of sonic test equipment	8. Demonstrate basic understanding of material hardness testing equipment

	1	2	3	4	5	6	7	8	9	10
I. EXPLAIN LOCAL PROCESS	1. Demonstrate understanding of overall operation and critical path	2. Demonstrate ability to set priorities	3. Demonstrate understanding of component operation	4. Demonstrate understanding of operational standards	5. Demonstrate understanding of maintenance standards	6. Demonstrate ability to perdict time and man-power needed for repairs	7. Arrange for interdepartment cooperation i.e., job site areas	8. Demonstrate basic understanding of quality control	9. Demonstrate use of "dye checks," and magnaflux	10. Demonstrate basic knowledge of optic measuring equipment
J. DEMONSTRATE KNOWLEDGE OF LUBRICANTS	1. Demonstrate basic understanding of lubricant theory	2. Demonstrate basic understanding of lubricant systems	3. Demonstrate basic understanding of different lubricants	4. Use lubricant code books	5. Demonstrate basic understanding of oil recovery systems	6. Demonstrate basic understanding of filters and micron sizes	7. Demonstrate basic understanding of product lubricant	8. Demonstrate basic understanding of hazards of various fluids and lubricants	9. Demonstrate basic understanding of compatability of fluids, lubricants, hoses, resevoirs, etc.	

PANEL MEMBERS — Bethlehem Steel Corporation

David M. Hill
Dave Kelly
Bud Lykes
Clifton W. Maiden
Walter S. McClusky

C. L. Meadows
Roy von Nordeck
Charles T. Pickett
Robert E. Schmidt
Roger K. Shackelford

C. W. Taylor
Matt Wilson
William C. Wright

Recorder

Irene Boyce

DACUM Facilitator

Jack Harris, Stark Technical College/Synectic Management

world situation. Equally, the company representatives found it intriguing to take actual job knowledge and relate it to the educational process. Both groups had to take time out to explain company or educational jargon to one another, and both groups derived pleasure from being able to adopt quickly the other's jargon.

After two days of learning the DACUM approach and conceptualizing the needs of the Inspector-Planner Program, the group spent two additional days of intensive work assigning the 126 competencies to a group of courses. In some cases, these courses already existed at the college and were utilized with minor modifications. Most of the courses (approximately 90 percent), however, were developed specifically for the program. Utilization of a more traditional curriculum development format probably would have taken an entire semester. This approach, from competency identification to identification of the course of study, took one week—one very intensive week (Bruns, 1983)!

Using these competencies, the college's Counseling and Testing Division determined the math and reading levels required for the program. Special assessment instruments were designed so that they only measured items that were related to the job. Employees not passing the initial preassessment could sign up for a two-week brush-up course and take the assessment a second time. This provision was made because the program involved many employees who had been out of school for as many as twenty-five years. After taking the first assessment, the employees identified as needing more than a brush-up were offered the opportunity to take semester-long remedial courses to upgrade their skills for future training sessions.

Anxiety among the workers applying for the program was extremely high, since rumors had circulated that the test was designed to keep most of the eligible employees out of the Inspector-Planner Program. Once the actual test had been given, the anxiety level was reduced as it became apparent that the test was not designed to be a selection tool but merely to provide a cutoff for the skill level needed for success in the college program. The college also met with union officials from both the local and the international union to explain the reason for the test and what the tests were designed to do.

Since the community college has become the work station for Bethlehem Steel employees, several other problems have developed. While both the faculty and the company are committed to turning out the highest caliber of trained employees, the company's expenditure of considerable sums of money created a need on its part for some early termination procedures. Since the faculty have an ongoing commitment to doing whatever is possible to help students achieve, regardless of time or cost, those procedures were an anathema. This problem (along with others) was solved simply by allowing the faculty, company, and union representatives to discuss it and determine how all sides could effectively deal with it. The ability to work together is one of the outstanding benefits of a program of this type, and the cooperation has extended into new areas where it previously had not occurred. Faculty, for the first time, were able to obtain the cooperation of a major corporation in providing equipment, technology, and, most of all, the information that is needed to enhance existing courses. Working with this innovative program greatly enhanced faculty morale.

Since selection for the program is based upon seniority, once the criteria had been met successfully, the first twenty-five inspector-planners to arrive at Dundalk Community College had an average of thirty years with the company. Consequently, the college realized that the transition from steel mill to college student for these workers would be a major one. The company and college planned a three-day orientation for the group. The orientation ranged from team-building skills to an understanding of the college's grading system. Included in the orientation was a one-day tour of the Sparrows Point plant because, while these employees had spent thirty years ther;e, most of them had never seen the complete steel-making process.

The college faculty also participated either in this tour or in a previous "behind-the-scenes tour" arranged just for them. The three-day orientation ended with a reception for the inspector-planners and their wives on the last evening. Prior to the reception, the wives and men went through a counseling brainstorming session to look at the possible changes that their lives would undergo in the next thirty weeks. As an outgrowth of these meetings, the wives requested additional sessions as the semester unfolded. Also, some of the wives have expressed interest in signing up for course work at the college.

The first group has completed the two-semester program. Of the twenty-five who started, two decided to return to the plant before the first eight-week termination period, and the remainder of the class successfully completed the program. The second class lost one member after the initial two-day orientation, with no other dropouts to date. A new group will begin every sixteen weeks until 200 to 300 individuals are trained. We expect things to be smoother with the succeeding groups because both the employees applying for the program and the instructors have a better idea of what to expect.

Future Direction and Applications

The success of DACUM for operational maintenance has served as a basis for the college deciding the following:

- All career-oriented programs will be reviewed and redefined on a competency basis over a two-year period by utilizing the DACUM approach

- All new programs in the design and development phase will be developed using DACUM
- At least eight faculty members from selected disciplines will be trained as DACUM facilitators, thereby reducing the need for outside technical assistance and further developing our response capability; this effort is nearly complete.

With the success of this program and approach, additional opportunities have been realized. Specifically, the college has developed a customized Master Maintenance Mechanics Program for W. R. Grace Corporation and designed a competency-based Master Millwright Program for Eastern Stainless Steel Corporation. Negotiations are underway to develop a competency-based First-Line Supervisory Development Program for the Sparrows Point plant. There are over 500 first-line supervisors at the plant, which will ensure a steady flow of students into the program in the years ahead.

A unique effort has also been underway to examine how the DACUM process could be utilized to revitalize our arts and science two-year curriculum program. A DACUM workshop has been held and specific competencies have been identified. Some follow-up validation will be conducted with selected field reviewers representing four- and two-year college faculty in selected discipline clusters. We look forward to the final results.

It is also my feeling that the DACUM customized curriculum development effort has other and possibly more significant applications. As Figure 2 suggests, if better methods of articulation of credit for training can be developed, the potential for an enhanced relationship between the educational and industrial sectors can be realized to each side's benefit. The DACUM approach is at least one way in which we can document clearly the type of training that specific industries require, but it can also be utilized as a means of documenting what is already taking place. If we are committed to determining the same level of specificity for our own programs, then linking the training elements together through close collaboration can serve as an "access" model for working adults that accommodates not only their needs for career and personal development but also business and industry's needs for a broader array of training services and technical assistance.

References

Adams, R. E. *DACUM: Approach to Curriculum, Learning, and Evaluation in Occupational Education.* Nova Scotia, Canada: Department of Regional Economic Expansion, 1975.

Figure 2. Linking Business and Industry
to Educational Opportunities

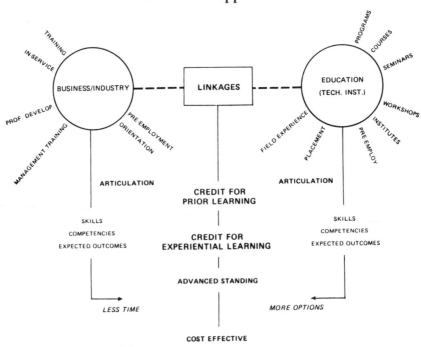

Source: Dundalk Community College

Bethlehem Steel. *Operation Maintenance Procedural Manual.* Baltimore, Md.: Bethlehem Steel, Sparrows Point plant, 1982.

Bruns, J. "Industrial Training: A Case Study." Paper presented at the National Center for Issues in Higher Education's National Conference, Dallas, Texas, Sept. 1983.

Carnavale, A., and Goldstin, J. *Employee Training: Its Changing Role and Analysis of New Data.* Washington, D.C.: American Society of Training and Development, 1983.

Chavez, L. "Iron and Steel Institute." *The New York Times,* June 20, 1982, p. 15.

Chavez, L. "The Year the Bottom Fell Out for Steel." *The New York Times,* June 20, 1982, p. 1, 15.

Ellison, N., and others. "Putting America Back to Work—A Partnership Approach to Economic and Human Resource Development." AACJC First Annual Report, Spring 1983, p. 2.

Hoffman, M., and Schwartz, G. *Economic Adjustment Strategies for Baltimore County, Maryland, 1983–1990.* Morton Hoffman and Company, 1982.

Miller-Beach, A. *DACUM: Identifying Competencies.* Columbus: Ohio State University, National Center for Research in Vocational Education, 1980.

Trautlein, D. H. "Bethlehem Steel Modernizes for the Future." Bethlehem, Pa.: News Media Division, Public Affairs, 1981.

Philip R. Day, Jr., is president of Dundalk Community College in Maryland.

*North Carolina's state-supported programs linking
community colleges to industrial training needs provide
an example of successful government-education-industry
collaboration.*

North Carolina: A Statewide System of Training for New and Existing Industries

H. James Owen

North Carolina's fifty-eight community and technical colleges are the "presumptive deliverers of public postsecondary training designed to meet the needs of individuals, business, and state development objectives," as outlined in an executive order by Governor James B. Hunt, Jr. (1983, p. 1).

Governor Hunt had indicated in 1981 that the state's community and technical colleges are "the backbone of our economy." He went on to note that community and technical colleges were the most important single element in his program of economic development.

This chapter reviews several areas included in the North Carolina statewide economic development strategy: cooperative skills training

This chapter is based upon presentations made to the American Association of Community and Junior Colleges (AACJC) Council on Occupational Education in 1981 and AACJC National Council on Community Services and Continuing Education in 1982.

R. Kopecek, R. Clarke (Eds.). *Customized Job Training for Business and Industry.*
New Directions for Community Colleges, no. 48. San Francisco: Jossey-Bass, December 1984.

centers, state priority programs, new and expanding industry training, and state legislative support. Strategies that have been successful nationally will also be reviewed.

Cooperative Skills Training Centers

The purpose of establishing cooperative skills training centers was to allow local institutions and industries to assess cooperatively local training needs and to develop instructional programs that are uniquely designed to respond to these needs. The nature and scope of the training might vary; however, the training centers were directed toward the needs of the production and manufacturing industries with particular emphasis on the occupations of industrial maintenance, machinist, and tool and die making. These programs were of particular importance to existing industries that needed specific skill training for a small group of employees.

The state legislature granted $75,000 per institution per year in special funds for cooperative skills training centers at eight institutions in 1981–82 and fifteen institutions during fiscal year 1982–83. The greatest need for training was in updating the skills of existing employees in the areas of electricity and electronics, particularly relating to trouble-shooting motor controls, programmable controllers, and microprocessor controls. There was also a continuing need to upgrade the skills of machinists, tool and die makers, and industrial maintenance personnel.

The following institutions were approved for cooperative skills training centers in 1982–83:

- Catawba Valley Technical Institute
- Cleveland County Technical Institute
- Coastal Carolina Community College
- Davidson County Community College
- Forsyth Technical Institute
- Guilford Technical Institute
- Halifax Community College
- Lenoir Community College
- Mitchell Community College
- Piedmont Technical College
- Pitt Technical Institute
- Robeson Technical Institute
- Rowan Technical Institute
- Wake Technical Institute
- Wilkes Community College

The following types and numbers of industries received training through cooperative skills training centers during 1982–83:

Types of Industries Served	Number of Industries
Furniture Manufacturing	101
Textile and/or Apparel Manufacturing	92
Metalworking Trades	54
Electrical/Electronic Companies	50
Miscellaneous Manufacturing (includes paper, chemical, rubber, plastics, wood, pharmaceuticals, and food processing)	44
Other Trades and Occupations	40
Construction Trades	30
Public Service (includes utilities, hospitals, transportation, and banking)	13
Total	424

The number of people who received instruction through cooperative skills training centers during 1982–83 totaled 3,451 in eight occupational areas:

Occupations	Number of Trainees
Production Managers and Supervisors	927
Industrial Maintenance Workers (includes mechanics, plumbers, pipe fitters, machine fixers, and HVAC mechanics)	802
Machinist and Tool and Die Makers	531
Production Workers (includes machine operators, tile setters, assemblers, forklift operators)	442
Electrical/Electronic Occupations	227
Product Distributors (includes sales, warehousing, shipping, receiving, and truck traffic controllers)	226
Engineering Technicians (includes drafters, designers, and quality assurance analysts)	175
Metal Fabrication Workers	121
Total	3,451

Instruction was offered in eight broad areas with some employees involved in more than one skill area during 1982–83:

Type of Skills Taught	Number of Trainees
Industrial Maintenance and Production-Related Training	1,261
Supervisory Training	549
Electrical/Electronic Skills	506
Metalworking and Related Skills	457
Management Information	406
Microprocessor and Computer Applications	386
General and Job-Related Instruction	375
Total	3,940

A total of 309 training classes were taught during 1982–83. Approximately 51 percent of the training was conducted at the institution and the remaining 49 percent took place at an industrial site. The number of classes conducted by individual cooperative skills training centers ranged from six to fifty-one with the average number being twenty-one classes per center. The shortest course reported was two hours in length and the longest 440 hours. Twenty-four courses were longer than 100 clock hours, but the majority were between twenty-four and sixty-six hours in length.

The large number of different skills taught and the varied organizational and instructional methods used reflect the philosophy and intent of this program.

State Priority Programs

The state legislature allocated $1.2 million for each year of the 1981–1983 biennium for equipment and operating costs for state priority programs. The money was earmarked for programs new to an institution as well as for enriching and upgrading existing programs in priority areas. The state board of community colleges approved $42,277 per program per year for each of thirty programs. The programs identified as high-cost, state priority, critical-need programs included instrumentation technology, industrial maintenance technology, chemical technology, machinist, and computer programming.

The state board of community colleges established basic criteria for the distribution of the funds for these programs. Individual institutions requesting the funds were required to provide: statements emphasizing the need for the specific programs; descriptions of job titles; expected employment opportunities for graduates of the programs;

projected number of students to be served; existing training and educational opportunities; program balance; and advisory and agency involvement. The prefunding of start-up costs for new programs along with the funds for enriching or upgrading existing programs of a state-priority nature have been extremely helpful to community and technical colleges in carrying out their role as the state's presumptive deliverer of skilled training. An overview of these programs from 1981 through 1984 is shown in Figure 1.

New and Expanding Industry Training

Nearly $11 billion in new and expanding industry investments and more than 170,000 new jobs have been announced for the state during the period 1977–1982. It is the role of the Department of Community Colleges' new and expanding industry program to assist these industries in training new production employees for specific job skills. This program is provided with state funds and is offered at little or no cost to the industry. The job of this program is to provide people who are trained to company specifications and who will be ready for employment when an industry opens its doors for production.

The cost of training is going up with the shift to high-technology programs. When the new and expanding industry program began over twenty years ago, the bulk of the training was generally in traditional industries such as agriculture, textiles, and furniture. Now approximately two-thirds of the training is in the areas of metals, metals fabrication, electronics, and chemicals.

Providing skilled manpower for both new and expanding industry is one of the community college system's major responsibilities. Closely linked to the state's economic development efforts, the system operates an array of programs to foster industrial growth, an arrangement that has focused national attention on North Carolina's ability to meet the demands of business and industry for skilled workers and that has established the program as a model for training.

During the last decade, there has been a change in North Carolina's job training marketplace as new industries have moved into the state and as existing industries have expanded and changed direction. Figures from the Department of Community College's Industry Services Division show, for example, that in 1971–72, 61 percent of the new and expanding industry training projects related to textile, food, and wood products industries. About 22 percent were for high-technology industries such as fabricated metals, electronic machinery, and transportation equipment industries. Ten years later, in 1981–82,

Figure 1. North Carolina Department of Community Colleges State Priority (Critical-Need) Programs: 1981–1984

Program Name	(Program No.)	1981–82 Additional Programs to System	1982–83 Additional Programs to System	1983–84 Additional Programs to System	1982–83 Upgrading of Existing Programs in System	1983–84 Upgrading of Existing Programs in System	Existing Programs as of June 30, 1983, in System
Electronic Eng. Tech	(T-045)	6		2	3	10	40
Machinist	(V-032)	2			5	7	39
Industrial Maint. Tech	(T-119)	4	1		1		11
Indus. Maint. (Electromc.)	(V-028)	8			1		25
Electronic Data Proc.	(T-022)	3			3		45
Instrumentation Tech.	(T-048)		3				8
Nursing	(T-059) & (T-116)		2		6		42
Chemical Technology	(T-037)		2				5
Industrial Mechanics	(V-033)				3		10
Electromechanical Tech.	(T-039)			1			4
Mechanical Eng. Tech.	(T-051)					2	8
Mech. Draft. & Design	(T-043)					5	20
Manufacturing Eng. Tech.	(T-050)					1	6
Automation/Robotics Tech.	(T-173)			1			None
Microelectronics Tech.	(T-174)			1			None
Totals		23	8	5	22	25	

Source: 1981–84 Minutes of the North Carolina Department of Community Colleges.

the figures show the opposite: 61 percent in high-technology areas and 23 percent in textile and related industries.

The figures also show that training people for high-technology occupations is more costly. In 1971–72, when the higher percentage of training projects concerned textile and related industries, the cost per trainee was $93.18. With the shift to high-technology training programs, the cost per trainee during 1981–82 was $383.89. The total cost of training in 1981–82 for all areas was $2.2 million.

During the 1983–84 fiscal year, 35 percent of the training programs were in the coastal areas of the state, 42 percent in the piedmont, and 23 percent in the mountains.

All training programs are administered by a local institution (a community college, a technical college, or a technical institute) serving the area in which the industry is located. Local administration ensures constant attention and a prompt response to industry needs. Within the North Carolina Department of Community Colleges there is one entire division, the Industry Services Division, dedicated exclusively to developing industrial training. The Industry Services Division is staffed by professionals experienced in helping the institutions design and operate customized training programs for new and expanding manufacturing companies.

The Industry Services Division is financed solely by the state of North Carolina. There are no federal funds involved. The North Carolina legislature appropriates state money directly to the state board of community colleges for the exclusive purpose of providing this training service to the state's new and expanding manufacturing industries.

The state provides all necessary instructors. If a company prefers to use some of its own personnel as instructors, the state still pays the salaries of all instructors.

The resources of the Industry Services Division are available to any new or expanding manufacturing employer creating a minimum of twelve new production jobs in North Carolina and to any new or prospective employee referred for training by the participating company or its employment agent.

The basic purpose of the industrial training service is to encourage companies to create more jobs in North Carolina. Therefore, the state-sponsored training may continue as long as the company continues to create new jobs in numbers sufficient to justify the investment of training funds. There are no arbitrary limits on a company's eligibility.

Most often classes are conducted on the sponsoring college's campus or at the company's plant. If neither of these alternatives is practical, state funds may be used to lease adequate training space in the community.

The state provides standard equipment normally associated with vocational and technical training (lathes, welding machines, measuring instruments, oscilloscopes, and so on). However, the company is expected to furnish any equipment specialized to its particular products or processes.

North Carolina's industrial service offers multiple employment-enrollment options not typically found in other states. Employees may be trained before they are hired (pre-employment training), after they are hired (postemployment training), or under any combination of these two modes. This versatility is one of the features that enables North Carolina's training service to respond to almost any situation. Experienced industrial training specialists help each company select the approach that best suits its particular circumstances.

North Carolina's industrial training service makes a conscious effort not to infringe on a company's right of selection. At a company's request, however, the Employment Security Commission will test and screen job candidates. Those applicants meeting the criteria established for a particular job are referred to the company for further evaluation.

The versatility of North Carolina's industrial training service is virtually unlimited. Because of its inherent flexibility, this service can accommodate almost any type of production job. Any job that can be defined can be arranged into a logical learning sequence.

Figure 2 indicates a ten-year comparison of types of training provided by type of company.

State Legislative Support

The year 1981 was proclaimed as the "Year of the Community College" in North Carolina. The year's biggest challenge was securing the $33 million of documented equipment needed to bring existing technical and vocational programs up to minimum levels. These needs had been documented recently through institutional surveys. Governor Hunt's (1981) proclamation pointed out the community and technical college system's contributions to the economic development of the state and to the quality of life of its citizens. In talks with business and industry leaders, speeches to the state legislature, and interviews with news media across the state, the governor focused on the system's critical need for dollars to repair and replace outdated and, in some cases, World War II vintage training equipment.

Governor Hunt and the state board of community colleges chairman Carl Horn (chairman of the board and chief executive officer of Duke Power Company) also launched a concerted effort to encourage business and industry to donate or allow on-site use of equipment for

Figure 2. A Ten-Year Comparison of Training Provided to New and Expanding Companies in Selected Industrial Categories

Fiscal Year	Appropriations to Department	Allotments to Institutions	Total No. Projects	Total No. Trainees	Cost per Trainee	Textile, Food, and Wood Products			Fabricated Metals, Machinery, Electronic and Transportation Equipment			Capital Investment by New and Expanding Industries (Calendar Year)
						No. of Projects	Percent of Total	Average Hourly Production Wage	No. of Projects	Percent of Total	Average Hourly Production Wage	
1970–71	$ 728,000	$ 918,286[a]	92	9,855	$93.12	56	61	$2.28	20	22	$2.81	$ 631,954,000 (1970)
1975–76	728,000	726,919	66	6,431	113.03	28	42	3.26	21	32	4.01	701,286,000 (1975)
1980–81	1,786,552	1,651,742	80	4,003	412.63	16	20	4.96	48	60	6.14	2,240,196,000 (1980)

[a] Received supplemental appropriations of $200,000

Source: North Carolina Department of Community Colleges, 1982.

training, an appeal that at best has provided up to 5 percent of what the system needs; public funds are needed for the vast majority of equipment needs. At the same time, letters from the North Carolina Department of Revenue were received outlining tax benefits to business for the loan of an employee or piece of equipment to a community college.

The effort began to pay off in the 1981–1983 biennium when the stage legislature appropriated $5 million in new equipment funds for the community college system. In addition, in September 1981, the system received its first major donation through this program—$50,000 worth of drafting equipment from IBM Corporation. Other businesses have now donated approximately $4.5 million worth of equipment and materials for the system. Since the equipment came very rapidly, the community college system established a warehouse in Raleigh to stock the donations so that individual colleges could order and pick up from one location.

The 1983 state legislature did a fine job in continuing to support community and technical colleges with special emphasis on equipment. The state budget for community and technical colleges was increased $25 million for 1983–84 as compared with 1982–83. For 1983–84, over $7.5 million of this increase was in *new* money earmarked for new vocational and technical equipment. The $15 million appropriation of new equipment money for 1983–1984 along with the $5 million of *new* money for 1981–1983 and with $4.5 million in donations from business and industry will go far in meeting the current equipment needs of North Carolina's community and technical colleges.

In addition, the state general assembly waived fees for students enrolled in new and expanding industry training; this gives added support to efforts to assist industry. Furthermore, it waived fees for all persons in adult basic education and in adult high school and GED (general education development) classes, feeling that every North Carolinian, regardless of age, should be able to receive education through the high school level without having to pay tuition. During 1982–83, over 20 percent of the high school diplomas awarded in North Carolina were awarded through the community college system. The balance were awarded through regular high school programs. In addition, approximately 34,000 students were enrolled in adult basic education courses during 1982–83 in the community college system.

Successful Elements Nationally

The reports of the many exemplary programs and practices of industry and education collaboration across the country were analyzed by Warmbrod, Persavich, and L'Angelle (1981) to ascertain what made them successful, the common elements that successful programs shared, and the distinct qualities of successful programs. The practitioners involved with these programs were asked to identify the critical elements for success in their programs. Common elements of successful economic development in North Carolina were outlined in a separate study by Clary and Iverson (1983). Many of the elements deemed successful in North Carolina were very similar to those found beneficial on a national basis. The following eleven elements summarize the characteristics of successful industry-education collaboration as found in the national study (Warmbrod, Persavich, and L'Angelle, 1981):

1. There must be good, clear communication among key persons in industry and education.
2. Excellence in teaching is essential.
3. There must be institutional flexibility in meeting the needs of industry.
4. Programs offered must be of high quality.
5. Good, active advisory committees are important.
6. Education should have a quick response time in meeting industry needs.
7. There must be recognition of mutual need.
8. The support of administrators and faculty within the college is required to serve industry successfully.
9. Careful and thorough planning in each cooperative effort is essential.
10. A clearly written agreement or contract helps achieve successful completion of joint endeavor.
11. There should be continued evaluation of the program to update and improve it.

Conclusion

North Carolina's statewide system of education and training for economic growth and development through the community college system works. It works because a wide variety of people work together on this goal as one of the most important ones for North Carolina. The attitude of governmental leaders toward business and toward the role that community and technical colleges play in job training and economic development is a very important ingredient for success. It is not likely that many states will be able to duplicate all of the successful elements of business, government, and education that do and have existed in North Carolina for many years, but our overall success boils down to teamwork — all elements working together toward the common goal of economic development for North Carolina.

66

References

Clary, J. R., and Iverson, M. J. *Maximizing Responsiveness to Industry by North Carolina Technical and Community Colleges.* Raleigh: North Carolina Department of Community Colleges, 1983.

Hunt, J. B., Jr. Speech given to the North Carolina State and Community College System meeting, Raleigh, 1981.

Hunt, J. B., Jr. *Executive Order 92: North Carolina Job Training Policy.* Raleigh, N.C.: Office of the Governor, 1983.

North Carolina Department of Community Colleges. *Answers About Industrial Training.* Raleigh: North Carolina Department of Community Colleges, 1982.

Warmbrod, C. P., Persavich, J. J., and L'Angelle, D. *Sharing Resources: Postsecondary Education and Industry Cooperation.* Research and Development Series No. 203. Columbus: Ohio State University, National Center for Research in Vocational Education, 1981.

H. James Owen is president of Tri-Cities State Technical Institute in Tennessee.

The provision of state funds for the development of contract courses at community colleges in New York has led to increased worker productivity and enhanced college-employer relations.

Worker Education for Improved Productivity: The Role of New York State Community College Contract Courses

W. Gary McGuire

In 1981, New York State, in order to promote greater involvement of its thirty community colleges in economic development, funded a $3 million three-year project to help community colleges initiate training contracts with local businesses. During the first two years of this project, over 450 companies were served by 345 contract courses. This chapter describes the involvement of New York's community colleges, including a case study of a statistical process control course.

New York State Community College Contract Course Legislation

Legislation enacted in 1948 created community colleges in New York State. A few years later, these colleges became part of the newly formed State University of New York (SUNY). The community colleges were founded as part of the state's commitment to increasing

R. Kopecek, R. Clarke (Eds.). *Customized Job Training for Business and Industry.*
New Directions for Community Colleges, no. 48. San Francisco: Jossey-Bass, December 1984.

access to higher education. Over the years, New York community colleges have enlarged their role in serving business and industry; however, the desire to be of even more service was thwarted by a state regulation that prohibited colleges from receiving any state assistance for courses provided for specific groups and not open to the public.

Community colleges are funded by three major funding sources: state aid, which equals approximately 34 percent of community college revenue; student tuition, which is currently limited to a maximum of 33 percent of budget revenue; and local tax support, which normally picks up the balance of an individual college's revenue. Funding from the state is based on a college's full-time equivalent (FTE) enrollment and currently is approximately $1,000 per FTE. An FTE in New York is equivalent to thirty student credit hours and is supported from all sources at about $3,000 per year. FTE enrollment is calculated on a three-year weighted average rather than on actual enrollment for the year to which funding is applied. The average provides a cushion in years two and three to a college that experiences a decline in year one. Most community colleges in New York have experienced consistent rising enrollments, so this formula results in underfunding.

In 1980, the expanding role of New York State community colleges and the restrictive nature of the funding formula prohibiting tax assistance for contract courses led to the enactment of legislation encouraging community colleges to contract specific training for local businesses and industries to allow these courses to be used in the funding formula for state aid. The legislation provides that state aid be paid for the entire FTE enrollment in contract courses rather than for the weighted average typically used. The legislation also allows contract course expenses to be funded by a combination of company fees and state aid. This means contract course expenses do not have to be budgeted in advance but rather are approved as individual contracts are negotiated. The enabling legislation holds that contract course costs shall include costs for "courses offered for the purposes of providing occupational training or assistance to businesses for the creation, improvement, and retention of job opportunities, through contract arrangements between a community college and a business, labor organization, or not-for-profit corporation, including management committees composed of labor, business, and community leaders organized to promote labor management relations, productivity, quality of working life, industrial growth, and retention of business in the community" (New York State Education Law, 1984).

In 1981, the first year of this legislation, 109 New York State businesses contracted for 172 courses. The following year, the program served 362 businesses with 173 courses, operating 1,031 FTEs and serving 16,931 people. Figure 1 shows the ten most popular courses offered to industries in the state in 1982–83.

Contract course legislation was initially approved for a three-year period as an experiment. Also, it limited state support of the program to $1 million annually. The 1984 New York State budget proposal included a renewed funding for contract courses with an increased annual appropriation to $1.5 million.

The Statistical Process Control Concept

In recent years, New York companies discovered that Japanese products were consistently superior in cost and quality to their own. Factors such as social attitudes, government operation, and group psychology are often credited with producing this superiority. But another important factor has been identified that impacts directly on both quality and productivity. After World War II, the noted American statistician, Dr. W. Edward Demming, taught Japanese management to use statistical process control to improve quality and reduce manufacturing costs. The statistical process control concept involves preventing the manufacture of defective parts instead of detecting defective parts once they have been produced. The cost of detection systems can be astronomical. Between 15 and 40 percent of the cost of manufacturing any product is caused by failure to make it right the first time. The economic relationship of quality and productivity is powerful, and the opportunity for change is great.

Because of this, New York State community colleges are involved in a major retraining program aimed at improving quality, productivity, and competitive position by helping companies adopt process control methods. Many companies are demanding that their suppliers do the same, and so the colleges are working with vendors as well. In 1982–83, the most heavily enrolled contract course in the state was that on statistical process control. Most of these courses are part of an overall training program of the companies for whom the courses are provided. These training programs are expected to accomplish the following:

- Produce management understanding of new economic realities, commitment to new philosophies, leadership in changing business practices and work environments, and the development of new management skills and attitudes
- Adoption of new methods and techniques for improving quality and productivity, removal of barriers to improvement, and utilization of employee commitment to quality

Figure 1. Ten Most Popular Contract Courses Offered by New York State Community Colleges in 1982–1983

Course Title	Community College	Company	Total Enrollment
1. Statistical Process Control	Adirondack Com. Col. Erie Com. Col. Finger Lakes Com. Col. Jamestown Com. Col. Monroe Com. Col. Niagara County Com. Col. Ulster Com. Col.	Hollingsworth & Vose Chevrolet Motor Div. Volplex Corporation Falconer Glass Ind. Rochester Form Machine Harrison Radiator Div. IBM	1,587
2. Cardiopulmonary Resuscitation (CPR)	Broome Com. Col. Duchess Com. Col. Hudson Valley Com. Col.	IBM IBM Highgate Nursing Home Norton Corp.	950
3. Financial Planning	Broome Com. Col.	IBM	942
4. Electrical Safety	Broome Com. Col.	IBM	746
5. Industrial Safety	Broome Com. Col. Finger Lakes Com. Col. Jamestown Com. Col. Monroe Com. Col. Ulster Com. Col.	IBM Hartman Engineering Jamestown Management Assoc. Rochester Products Div. Assoc. for Retarded Children	384

Course	Colleges	Companies	
6. Time Management	Corning Com. Col.	Thatcher Glass Corporation	
	Monroe Com. Col.	Rochester Gas & Electric Corp.	
		Rochester Products Div.	
		Sybron/Nalge	
	Tompkins-Cortland Com. Col.	Cortland Memorial Hospital	
	Ulster Com. Col.	IBM	351
7. Professional Skills Development	Duchess Com. Col.	IBM	305
8. Principles of Supervision	Jamestown Com. Col.	Jamestown Metal Corp.	
		Falconer Glass	
		Bush Industries	
	Jefferson Com. Col.	Phillip's Cable Man. Co.	
	Monroe Com. Col.	WXXI-FM	
		Community Savings Bank	
	Rockland Com. Col.	Orange & Rockland Inc.	
	Westchester Com. Col.	Empire of America	246
9. Stress Management	Broome Com. Col.	IBM	
	Corning Com. Col.	Thatcher Glass	
	Hudson Valley Com. Col.	Jamestown Man. Assoc.	
		Olean Homemaker's Service	
	Jamestown Com. Col.	Chatauqua Opportunities, Inc.	
	Monroe Com. Col.	R. T. French Co.	
	Niagara County Com. Col.	Nurses United	210
10. Word Processing	Corning Com. Col.	Thatcher Glass	
	Mohawk Valley Com. Col.	Oneida/Herkimer Consortium	
	Hudson Valley Com. Col.	St. Regis Paper Company	
	Rockland Com. Col.	Lederle Laboratories Corp.	167

- Sustained efforts to improve processes or products and services to reduce costs and to meet customer requirements.

Erie Community College, located in Buffalo, and Niagara County Community College, located fifteen miles north of Buffalo, have become heavily involved in statistical process control (SPC) instruction for two separate divisions of General Motors Corporation. The SPC courses are basically the same, although they are not provided under similar conditions. Erie Community College began its program in 1980 in conjunction with the development of a large, new Chevrolet engine production facility located in a suburb of Buffalo. The training project, entitled "Training for the Future," was unique for several reasons. The magnitude of the training effort was far greater than any other effort undertaken in western New York for a specific industry. The project involved 4,500 employees of the Chevrolet engine plant who were to receive all or part of a program designed to acquaint them with new techniques and technology to be used in the production of a new four-cylinder engine on a modernized engine assembly line. While all of the people in the project would not work on the assembly line, it was believed that the new technology would eventually have widespread application, so all 4,500 employees would benefit from this training program.

A second factor that made the "Training for the Future" project unique was the opportunity provided for industry and education to cooperate, setting the stage for other cooperative economic development projects in western New York. Segments of the training project were offered by Erie Community College, State University College at Buffalo, the State University of New York, University Center at Buffalo, Canisius College, and the Erie County Board of Cooperative Educational Services Occupational Training Center. The community college's segment of the training was financed through the New York State contract course legislation, while other parts of the project were funded through the Job Partnership Training Act, Vocational Education Act, and company fees. In addition to the SPC training, the project included instruction in metrics, motivational training, computer terminology, use of gauges, and tool changes.

Niagara County Community College's statistical process control instruction involved two types of courses, both connected to Harrison Radiator Division of General Motors Corporation and funded through the contract course program. Harrison Radiator Division, as Niagara County's largest employer, employs 7,000 people in several plants in Lockport, New York. The production facilities are located approximately ten miles from the college's main campus. Several years ago, the company began a quality circle program aimed at increasing employee morale and participation in production. The company also decided to design a technique that involved production workers directly in the discrimination of their product's quality. In 1983, Harrison chose to use statistical process control as the method of achieving this outcome, and the company contracted with the community college to provide the required instruction. The company took this approach because they discovered, like so many other firms, that community colleges can provide the training at lower cost and that this approach does not require the company to remove corporate employees from normal production and management responsibilities.

Of note is that the American Association of Community and Junior Colleges (AACJC) has joined in an effort with the Ford Motor Company and Jackson Community College in Michigan to train community colleges across the country in methods of teaching statistical process control. The result will more than likely be a large increase in SPC training programs provided by community colleges.

Course Development Procedures

Although three general approaches for developing training courses exist, New York State community colleges seem to prefer one of two approaches for developing contract courses. The first approach involves sending college staff to local industries to meet with personnel, training, and manufacturing representatives to learn about the companies' human resource development needs and the role that the college can play in satisfying them. At least four colleges have specialized positions for this function: Niagara County Community College, Monroe Community College, Mohawk Valley Community College, and Genesee Community College. In each case, these individuals report to the chief continuing education officer. At meetings with company representatives on site, college personnel learn about specific training needs that cannot be met through the regular curriculum and that require a custom-designed training program (or programs). The college representatives then return to the company with the faculty members who are able to address the training needs, and the faculty and company representatives develop appropriate courses.

An alternative approach is for colleges to put together "canned" training packages standardized to meet the needs most often requested. These "canned" programs are then described and "sold" to company officials. The third alternative is a combination of the first two. In these cases, custom-designed programs are developed and, when successful for one company, are standardized and sold, sometimes with modifications, to other firms.

74

Conclusion

New York State has recognized the value of placing resources at the disposal of its community colleges as incentives to increasing college-employer linkages for improved worker productivity. The value of this state priority becomes clear when one sees how instrumental it was in the development of statistical process control courses, which helped to improve the productivity of over 1,500 employees of seven different companies in courses provided by seven community colleges.

New York's experience should serve as an example of how a relatively simple, nonbureaucratic, low-cost, statewide program can have a profound impact on corporate training. The key to success is the existence of a ready delivery system, and, in most states, that system exists in their community colleges.

References

New York State Education Law. Chapter 762, Section 6304, Subsection 1.b.i, 1984. (Law revised in 1984.)

W. Gary McGuire is dean of community education at Niagara County Community College in New York.

The role training has played in improving productivity
at Corning Glass Works is described, and suggestions for
educators entering the "training business" are provided.

Partnerships for Employee Training: Implications for Education, Business, and Industry

David B. Luther

The education community in the United States is faced with an outstanding opportunity that is difficult to refuse but easy to misunderstand or mismanage. It is an opportunity that could have a major impact on the future growth and prosperity of the education profession. The opportunity does not reside in the more well-known areas of cooperation between industry and education, such areas as executive programs, corporate on-site degree programs, or research-based consortiums. Instead, it is based on the recognition by American industry that well-trained, involved, and highly motivated employees are a critical element of commercial success. Indeed, employee training to enhance performance and productivity is a major element required to reverse the United States' declining trend in industrial competition.

Education can and should play a dynamic role in this revitalization of the American work force. It is true that for years in many large American corporations employee training has been pointed to with pride as an employee right. But current attitudes in industry reflect a

R. Kopecek, R. Clarke (Eds.). *Customized Job Training for Business and Industry.*
New Directions for Community Colleges, no. 48. San Francisco: Jossey-Bass, December 1984.

change from regarding employee training and education as an employee right to seeing well-trained employees as a requirement of corporate success, equally important to (or more important than) state-of-the-art technology, automated factories, or even short-term financial brilliance. Education and training are no longer benefits to be offered simply to those who want them. They are a must for reaching the new standards of excellence required in most companies. The economic survival of many industries is dependent on how well they train their employees, and the education community must be prepared to respond to this ever-increasing need.

Sources of Change

We can identify five sources for this change in attitude toward employee training. The recession of 1982 was deeper and lasted longer than many of us guessed it would. The end of the recession has revealed a massive restructuring of industry: A few companies have ceased to exist. Some others will never return to their pre–1982 dominance. Many look substantially different than they did in the late 1970s with a much leaner work force. Brand-new companies and even industries have emerged with new demands and new opportunities. The recession has forced changes in industry to occur in months that normally would have taken years.

A second, somewhat older source of change is the inflation of the late 1970s that led us to believe we were doing well when, indeed, we were not. Increased prices obscured the fact that fundamental industrial processes were losing not only their competitive position but also their ability to be financially solvent in a tightened economy. Increased efficiency of world-class firms accentuated the decline of many American companies, but this was masked by inflation, which caused a false sense of security.

A third source is the change in the work force population: Large numbers of blacks, Hispanics, and women have entered the workplace with very appropriate demands for opportunity and reward. This has created an ever-expanding work force and a pressure to open all jobs to all citizens.

A fourth source is the information revolution, which seems to generate ninth-grade geniuses and manager-level computer illiterates. Corporations are being led into an advanced-technology revolution, in many cases, by managers who have a healthy fear of this same technology. Future managers will be required not only to be computer literate but they will also need to be computer managers.

The fiifth source is Japan, or at least what the name "Japan" signifies in the minds of many in industry—quality, lower prices, government assistance, and a unique culture that seems to make the impossible a rather common occurrence. Also, in the minds of some American businesspeople, the name generates fear, fear of what the Japanese phenomenon means to the long-term success of their companies and themselves.

I suggest that community colleges need to be concerned with only two of these sources of change in responding to the training needs of industry—Japan and the information revolution. The other sources will die or be replaced: The recession is over; inflation has dropped very dramatically; and changes in the work force continue but with, hopefully, improved means for satisfying those demands that today remain unanswered.

The Japanese Influence

Any discussion of Japan must center on the impression that a synonym for "Japan" is "quality." An expansion of the use of the word "quality" in industry is critical. Instead of thinking that quality means how long your toaster will last, expand the definition to encompass everything we do, from writing good memos, to responding quickly to a supervisor's request, to building a better automobile. Think of providing a "quality" work environment that allows and encourages every individual in that environment to reach his or her maximum potential. Japan has realized the essential role that training plays in achieving quality. Only when quality becomes pervasive can an organization start to achieve what Japan has accomplished with the goods and services they sell.

Can we do it? You bet we can! My experience is limited to Corning Glass Works, but let me give you an example. We make ceramic substrates for automotive emission control, the basis of the pollution control system for your automobile's exhaust. We invented the process; we shipped the first piece to Detroit; we achieved full-scale production; but, less than four years later, a Japanese company was supplying a better product at a lower price. They threatened to capture the whole market, which would have cost many Corning employees their jobs and caused equipment to become obsolete.

A very determined plant manager insisted on one more chance to improve Corning's competitive standing. He expanded training to unheard-of levels in his plant and solicited the involvement of every worker, including the sweeper and the file clerk. Because of training involvement and a lot of hard work, our workers learned how to do their job right the first time and we got the business back — in fact, we now ship to the Japanese auto industry.

Our quality goal for ceramic substrates is to produce no more than two bad parts per million shipped. We are meeting that goal. And everyone in that plant today has a new understanding of what quality means. Our experience taught us something else, which we should have known: Our workers want to do a good job, they want to be proud of their work, and they will do good work if management provides the tools, training, and leadership. The decline in quality in American industry is not a labor problem; it is a management problem.

Two ingredients for achieving quality are training and involvement. To involve people itself requires training — training that includes everyone from the top of the organization to the bottom and that goes on constantly. Training is not a pill to take and forget; it is more like breathing — a natural, ongoing process. Of course, there are other elements involved in achieving quality (communication and recognition systems, senior management involvement, and union cooperation), but employee training is the cornerstone, and industry will be looking to this nation's community college system to help provide it.

The Information Revolution

The information revolution has brought computer-aided design/computer-aided manufacturing CAD/CAM, office automation, desktop computers, personal computers, computer work stations, and teleconferencing into American businesses. At Corning Glass Works (CGW), computer terminals are everywhere. You have to be reasonably skilled even to use the new telephone services. How do people learn to use all this new technology? Through training. In fact, our recently retired chairman had to spend time in class to learn how to use a digital voice message recording feature on his new telephone. He was glad to do so because he learned he could talk to our entire North American management group with a single phone call. Training provided him with one more tool with which to deal with change.

Education's Opportunity

The industrial market for training, then, is both very large and very important. At CGW, our goal is to have employees spend 5 percent of their time being trained or educated; that is equivalent to an institution with 1,000 students all year long. Currently, American

companies spend $400 per year per employee on education and train-
ing or $30 billion per year total, according to *Cleveland Plain Dealer*
(1982). This base level will grow, presenting education with a marketing dream. In fact, if I were a venture capitalist, I would invest in the
best training and education development and delivery system I could
find. Many states believe that they have done exactly that through the
establishment and refinement of responsive community college
systems.

Problems to Be Overcome

This chapter opened with the statement that, in addition to having a great opportunity, education also faces potential misunderstand-
ing and mismanagement in the area of industrial training. Why isn't
education being overwhelmed with requests from industry for help? My
experience says there are several reasons:

1. Some companies have not really recognized the need for a
new understanding of an improvement in quality, and thus they have
not recognized the massive training required to support quality production.

2. Some businesses have had bad experiences in asking professional educators to provide employee training. Offering an off-the-shelf
version of "Business Administration 101" that has been acceptable for
years in the classroom has failed miserably when it has not been what
the customer wanted or needed. Customized training programs that
respond to exact industry needs must become the operating mode of
the education community.

3. Professional educators frequently do not treat their customers as customers. Flexibility is lacking; knowledge of industry-specific
technology is occasionally not at the leading edge; no attempt is made
to get to know the customer or understand his or her real needs; little
attention is given to establishing trust and credibility.

4. On the part of industry, there is a tendency to underrate the
need for teaching skills, resulting in the primary emphasis in training
programs going to content and less emphasis going to effective delivery.

Suggestions for Educators

If educational institutions are to go into the corporate education
and training business, there are some guidelines that should be considered. I do not know a great deal about education, but I do know
something about business. Business is concerned with customers and

products and services and, of course, quality. I suggest that educators take the following steps in developing customized training programs:

1. Get to Know the Customer. Learn about the business, the products, and the competition. Read the annual reports. Read the credit reports. Officer biographies are public information—find out about the people you are dealing with. Find out who the customers are and who the suppliers are. See if there are published articles available. Is the business profitable or in Chapter 11? Is its market a mature or a new one? Is the product a commodity, or is a large share of the market based on a unique technology, product, or distribution system? Are there statements of business strategy available for you to read? To know the customer's needs, you must know the customer.

2. Learn About the Customer's Problems and Needs. Let him or her describe the company's problems and tell you what has worked or not worked before. Keep exploring—what you think you heard may not be what the customer thought he or she said the first time around. Understand what the customer is trying to do with training. Is it being established to satisfy a boss's request or a consultant's recommendation, or is it really to change the organization or meet a specific need? How is training currently accomplished? Is it in-house or vendor supplied? Is there a strategy? If an education and training department currently exists, to whom does it report in the company hierarchy? Who is the real decision maker? How is training funded?

3. Develop a Strategy for Satisfying the Customer's Need. Once you have helped a company identify a problem or a part of a problem you think you can do something about, do your homework. How will you satisfy the problem? What constitutes success? What are the details for delivery? What are the characteristics of those to be trained? Can you present alternatives to the customer? Do you know what you are talking about? How do you make the customer feel that he or she is really in charge? Finally, how do you describe all this so that the customer understands why you are the best choice to satisfy the company's training needs? Remember that the corporate training world is very competitive, and many private firms will be direct competitors of educational institutions as providers of training.

4. Do a Good Job. Ask for critiques along the way. Ensure that you do what you say you are going to do. Modify the program as needed and show that providing a quality training program is a top priority for your institution.

5. Follow Up. There are good salespeople that say the sale really begins after you get the order. Follow up and find out what went right and what went wrong (and something always goes wrong). Show willingness to change and learn from your first sale — you will want others. A successful program will lead to continued training with a company. One failure, early on, will effectively eliminate any chance for future cooperation.

These suggestions may sound like a quick course in basic salesmanship. They are. But American industry is very capable of finding other ways to fill their needs than through professional educators, and that, in my opinion, would be a real loss. The education community can take advantage of the opportunity corporate training offers, but it must make the first move.

Why Should Education and Industry Interact?

Many people ask why there should be a liaison between the education system and business and industry. The benefits of this alliance are obvious, but some specific industry advantages to cooperating with education are:

1. Educators know how to teach. This is a critical element that has been missing from many corporate training programs.

2. Customers (business and industry) can see real benefit from buying services and avoiding the fixed costs involved in hiring staff to do the teaching. It is financially viable to subcontract training to educational institutions.

3. Education can afford to specialize and become very expert in one or two fields. This is very tough to do with a corporate staff. By serving many companies, education can maximize its staffing and delivery of training programs.

4. Finally, the partnership allows professional educators to become involved in what promises to be a very exciting time for business in America.

References

"Nailing Down for Employment." *Cleveland Plain Dealer,* May 26, 1982.

David B. Luther is vice-president of the Quality, Consumer, and Industry Group at Corning Glass Works in New York.

Specific practices that help to ensure an institution's success
in industrial training are described.

Components of Successful Training Programs

Dorothy J. Kaplan

Education and training for business and industry require intense effort, emphasis on detail, and constant monitoring and evaluation. The foundation of successful programs rests on special attention to program components. Halfhearted responses by a college to its training programs will produce mediocrity and program stagnation or failure. This chapter outlines the essential components of successful training programs and details practices and techniques for those colleges beginning or expanding training services.

Institutional Commitment

An extensive program of business and industry training requires support from the college president, board of trustees, administration, and faculty. To maintain this support, the college must establish a communication network that includes all constituencies in order to foster a team concept and to ensure that the program has knowledgeable spokespersons and supporters throughout the institution. A monthly memorandum listing programs in the planning and initiation stages is

R. Kopecek, R. Clarke (Eds.). *Customized Job Training for Business and Industry.*
New Directions for Community Colleges, no. 48. San Francisco: Jossey-Bass, December 1984.

a minimum effort. Included in this memo should be information on all companies contacted and all work in progress. A brief update at trustee, administrative, and faculty meetings, reviewing accomplishments as well as plans, encourages positive relationships. Brief articles in house organs provide additional information to the entire college community.

The President's Role

In a study concerning service to industry conducted by the National Center for Research in Vocational Education (Warmbrod, Persavich, and L'Angelle, 1981), a critical element for success was found to be the strong leadership of the college president. A sucessful way of demonstrating this interest is for the president to sponsor break-fast or luncheon meetings with chief executive officers (CEOs) of local companies. Before and during the meal, company personnel can be introduced to the campus, given general information about the college's traditional programs, informed of the college as a business and industry training resource, and shown a brief, professionally prepared, audiovisual presentation. This presentation can emphasize the mission of the college, visually reinforce program highlights, and demonstrate the college's economic impact on the community. The total contact, including the served meal, should not exceed one hour.

Such a series of on-campus meetings requires careful planning and coordination. One chief executive officer should be scheduled at a time, and this individual should be invited to bring one or two staff people. From the college, in addition to the president, one or two people, such as the dean of the business division, the director of industrial programs, or the director of institutional advancement (whose office might handle the logistics of the meetings), should attend. The total group should not exceed six to eight people to allow for a free and easy exchange of ideas.

Since image building is an important goal of these meetings, thought should be given to the meal's setting and ambiance. First impressions are important. The menu obviously should be appropriate. Since time is also a critical element to success, prompt, professional, and unobtrusive service is essential. A small private dining room or a board room could provide an excellent setting for the meeting.

These meetings have several potential benefits. Most important is the general public relations value of exposing the company's CEO to the college, its programs, facilities, and personnel. The meeting gives the college president the opportunity to meet company personnel on the president's own turf in order to sell (however softly) college programs. Further, it provides company personnel with what may be their first opportunity to "buy into" their community college. By the use of a few simple leading questions, college personnel can learn much about the company, its history, current operations, and plans. The information gathered at these meetings can be of sufficient benefit to the college's planning process to justify the time spent on them, even if the gatherings produce few training prospects.

From a view of selling training, even more specific benefits can occur. The meeting may serve as a catalyst for the corporate president to crystallize vague ideas into firm action plans. If this happens, the college benefits because it becomes involved at the very beginning of the planning process. During the meal, the CEO will often specify the individual who should be contacted at the company to pursue future discussions. This opens the door for the initial, all-important, appointment at the business, and it also provides the publicly acknowledged backing of the company's president, which is invaluable.

In the worst-case scenario, if the company is absolutely not interested in training, the breakfast meeting saves the college staff time that might have been spent in proposal preparation, yet it ensures that company personnel know of the college's interest in the firm.

In the Warmbrod, Persavich, and L'Angelle (1981) analysis of successful elements in industry and education collaborative programs, foremost was the recognition that there must be good, clear communication among key persons in industry and education. To achieve this level of communication, industrial and educational personnel must understand each other's roles and responsibilities and what each can offer. Presidential breakfasts or luncheons are excellent opportunities to begin this communication link, but the process must be followed up at lower levels.

Practitioners in the Warmbrod, Persavich, and L'Angelle survey also concluded that a critical element for success is the support of administrators and faculty within the college. Administrators and faculty must see training programs as part of their institutional mission and recognize the benefits. The college president, by his or her interest and active involvement, establishes the context for this support.

Institutional Flexibility

Although educational institutions are not known for their flexibility and quick response to need, these attributes must be developed if a college is to be successful in training. Companies want everything yesterday and assume that anything necessary to their operation will be available by tomorrow at the latest.

The Warmbrod, Persavich, and L'Angelle survey contained two items related to flexibility. First, educational institutions should have a quick response time to meet the needs of industry. Quick response requires knowledgeable and skillful college personnel. These individuals must be capable of defining training needs based on an analysis of the required job or the specific instructions of company personnel, writing training plans, developing instructional material, recruiting staff, and pricing, implementing, and evaluating programs. Skill in developing courses also can help provide quick delivery and successful outcomes.

Second, there must be institutional flexibility in meeting the needs of industry. Such flexibility must extend to the scheduling of courses, assigning of faculty, and designating of locations where courses can be offered. Program times, length, and location must be consistent with the company's hours and needs. Flexibility is also needed in selecting the mode of instruction — that is, the delivery system (Pennsylvania Department of Education, 1983).

Instructors

The expertise of full-time faculty is of inestimable value in conducting training programs; however, because of industrial scheduling demands and the requirements of regular college schedules, full-time faculty are not often available. Therefore, the college must have at hand a cadre of training consultants who can serve as instructors. Most of these individuals are otherwise employed but available for short periods of time from their companies by utilizing such mechanisms as release time, vacations, off-shift time, or leaves of absence.

In addition to careful reviews of technical and teaching qualifications, all consultants should be interviewed to ascertain their enthusiasm and personality as well as their energy. It is highly desirable for the consultant to have work experience in the field. Nothing hurts the credibility of a program more than the presentation of "theory" without the reinforcement of practical experience.

In addition to using newspaper ads to identify qualified instructors, contact with local training and personnel directors will also often produce qualified candidates. These directors can usually be contacted through their professional associations. Professional organizations of accountants, attorneys, and data processors are also valuable sources of personnel for training programs in these fields.

Retirees are an additional source of qualified instructors. These motivated and enthusiastic individuals bring a wealth of information, skill, and knowledge to the classroom. They can be contacted through personnel offices of local firms or organizations for retired persons such as Service Corps of Retired Executive (SCORE) or the American Association of Retired Persons (AARP).

Needs Assessment

The training needs of every company are different. These needs traditionally are determined by conducting formal needs assessments. Observation, personal interviews, and questionnaires are utilized to accumulate the data necessary to construct a meaningful program.

This time-honored approach, however, may be changing. The State Technical Institute in Memphis, Tennessee, does not use formal needs assessment surveys. Their experience has shown that a company generally knows what it needs. In their technique, the institute personnel listen to company personnel, make suggestions, and then suggest class outlines or a curriculum. This informal approach to needs assessment, they report, has worked well for both the institute and its clients (Warmbrod and Faddis, 1983).

Basic Elements in the Development of Industrial Training Programs

All programs and courses, regardless of their sophistication, contain variations of the following elements. Since client satisfaction in the learning process is dependent on the attitudes and perceptions of the employee-students and the personnel of the firm, as well as on what, how much, and how well the employees learn and subsequently perform, each of the following elements requires careful attention and satisfactory completion.

Element 1. The company and the college must agree on the identification of the training need and the outcomes that are to occur from the program. The agreement (usually formally documented in some type of contract or memorandum of understanding) should specify the terms of the proposed program or course, including initial determinations of the type and scope of training, numbers of individuals to be involved, time, price parameters, evaluation methods, and provisions that specify the mechanism for both parties to agree to new or adjusted conditions to their contract.

Element 2. An instructor-trainer with the required experience, knowledge, and skills available during the time specified by the company must be identified. As will be explained in the next section, more sophisticated or larger programs with several components may use a curriculum specialist to conduct a task analysis and develop a training plan and curriculum. A program coordinator to administer, coordinate, and serve as a liaison between the company and the college may also be employed.

Element 3. A meeting between the instructor and company representatives is held for information gathering and to begin the specific course planning process. It is important for the instructor to speak to all individuals at the company directly related to the programs. During these conversations, the instructor can ascertain first hand the competencies needed to be learned as well as the skill levels of the participants to be taught. A visit to the work sites and observations of the company's ongoing operation are also important to instructional planning.

Element 4. The design and development of the course should be completed by the instructor whose knowledge of the subject area helps determine the course length and content. The resources of the college— library, audiovisual department, handouts, overhead transparencies, slides, course outlines, and test material—are made available to the instructor. Access to instructors in the same or related fields, if available, can also be a tremendous asset.

Element 5. Course outlines should be reviewed by appropriate college personnel and shared with company representatives. At this point the company has an opportunity to review the program and verify that the outline and the stated objectives will meet its specific needs.

Further Comments on Complex Programs

Programs that are complex require much more than course development by a single instructor. In these situations, formal task analysis and the development of a training plan by a knowledgeable curriculum coordinator are required. This individual meets with company representatives and develops a total program based on the required components. In some instances, this process could even involve the development of a training manual to serve as a text for the program. Obviously, fees for the curriculum coordinator, the development and printing of the manual, and all other such services are additional items to be funded.

Contracts

A clearly written agreement or contract is most helpful in achieving successful completion of training programs. When the duties and responsibilities of each party are clearly delineated, misunderstandings are reduced.

The controlling document can be as informal as a letter of understanding or as formal as a contract, but either should address the following points:

- *Program Title and Brief Description* — Paragraph giving program title, a description of the course content, and what is to be accomplished by whom
- *Schedule* — Dates and times the classes will take place
- *Physical Facilities* — Location of training site
- *Equipment* — List of special equipment required (such as projectors) and who is supplying it
- *Instructor* — Name of instructor and a brief biographical description highlighting his or her relevant experience
- *Number of Trainees* — Number of participants, including a minimum and maximum class size
- *Fee* — List including the components of the total figure, such as the tuition as agreed to earlier and any additional charges for curriculum, consultant, textbooks, meal charges
- *Method and Time of Payment* — Billing arrangements (for example, billed 50 percent at start of program and 25 percent at midpoint, or billed at conclusion of program) or any other specific arrangements to which the college and company have agreed. (If there is any penalty for cancellation of the program, or any other special considerations, the specifics should be included. This is particularly important where there is potential for the company to be forced to cancel the program after development but prior to presentation.)
- *Signatures* — Company and college representatives should sign and exchange copies of the agreed-upon document.

The format of the contract will depend on the policies and procedures of the individual institution. However, a standard methodology should be developed and used by all involved parties.

Instructor's Contract

To fix arrangements between the college and the instructor and to avoid misunderstandings, a contract or letter of understanding should exist that contains, at least, the following: name of the instructor; college name and name of contracting firm; program title and a brief description of course content; schedule of classes; address of specific training site(s); individual to contact at company, if necessary; projected number of trainees; list of equipment needed; obligations of instructor related to the development of course content and material; expected methods of evaluation of trainees, instructor, course, and program; salary; method and time of payment; and authorizing signatures.

Recognition

A certificate of attendance presented at the last class session, hopefully presented by the company representative, provides documentation of accomplishment. It is a vital part of every program.

In addition, the granting of continuing education units (CEUs) serves as an additional public relations tool. A national effort has been underway for several years to grant a form of credit for credit-free career training and lifelong learning. One CEU for every ten hours of training may be granted by an accredited institution for courses and/or experience that the accredited institution considers to be career applicable. Accrual of CEUs signifies professional development and provides a mechanism for recording these achievements.

Evaluations

Continual program evaluation in writing is essential for enhancing, updating, and improving its procedures and management. This assessment record allows for future tracking and planning based on specifics. Central to this process is an evaluation instrument to be filled in by each trainee. The information from these forms becomes a critique of the program content and individual presentations. The data should be shared with the company and used as a developmental tool in designing future programs. Student evaluations also serve as an evaluation of the instructor, which aids in making future assignments.

Courses that are based on specific skill development have a practical — and critical — test: the participant's mastery of the skill being taught.

In nontechnical programs, such as management development, it is difficult to measure immediate concrete results. In such cases, repeat business is one measure of a course or a center's success.

The written evaluation by the college of a program is useful in planning new projects, and it can serve as a "reference" when contacting new companies. In addition, the act of evaluation by the college demonstrates to the company that the institution is concerned about the quality of the program and its ability to meet the firm's objectives.

Mailing List

Mailing lists must be developed and continually edited. When possible, the name of a specific individual should be part of the address, but it is important to update these names as individuals change positions.

The most important list for community college training personnel contains the names of personnel directors at local companies. These names can sometimes be acquired from local chapters of American Society for Personnel Administration (ASPA) or ASTD, or they can be developed from a chamber of commerce mailing list or by going through the telephone book. Computerization of lists allows for easy subcategorization. Some of the subcategories found to be most useful include those that list personnel directors by industry or business (such as banks, manufacturing companies, retail establishments, and so on). Such subcategorization is helpful when offering seminars, workshops, and programs tailored to specific groups.

Organizational Contact

It is very important to have ongoing contact with local organizations, especially those comprised of business representatives, personnel managers, and training directors. It is not necessary to have one individual as a member of all organizations. With total faculty and staff knowledge of customized services, various individuals can belong to organizations and be responsible for spreading the word of program availability as well as bringing back leads of companies interested in programs. In addition, the exchange of information at such meetings allows the college to keep in touch with current business trends and developments.

Marketing the Program

A college cannot announce through the newspaper that training programs are available and then sit back waiting for calls. More aggressive steps are necessary. Personal contact with the personnel directors of area firms requesting an appointment is the first step. In these phone conversations, college personnel should stress the benefit to these personnel directors of participating in a brief meeting.

A mailing to companies explaining the college's available services may be another beneficial marketing approach. Triton College in Illinois, for example, sends a letter to a company president or director of training, opening with "Are you running a business or are you running a school?" It then goes on to introduce Triton's offer to conduct a training needs assessment for the company, at no cost or obligation to the firm, and extends an invitation to call the college or return an enclosed postage-paid card.

To companies who do not respond, Triton sends a follow-up letter (Warmbrod and Faddis, 1983) that begins:

> Dear Executive:
>
> I'd like to take this opportunity to compliment you. Your employee training programs must be operating at peak efficiency level... accomplishing all the things that you want them to.... *If these things weren't true, you'd be asking me to tell you more about Triton for training* (p. 142).

Marketing a college's capability to provide customized training is much like selling a product, so it is imperative that a marketing plan be developed and salesmanship skills be honed and utilized.

Conclusion

A successful business and industry training program requires total institutional commitment. The support of the chief executive officer is a critical element in achieving positive results.

Because business and industry require rapid decision making and scheduling, flexibility is necessary to offer services to this audience. This is not the operational norm at most postsecondary institutions; extra thought must be given to establishing a workable delivery system.

Instructors must have working industry experience, and course content must be relevant. In-house procedures must be established, and attention to detail is of vital importance.

A basic ingredient in program success is marketing. Business and industry services are competitively marketed, and it is necessary to establish procedures that will compete successfully. Such services must be perceived by industry as a major focus of the institution, not as an afterthought.

References

Pennsylvania Department of Education. *Supporting Economic Development: A Guide for Vocational Educators.* Harrisburg: Pennsylvania Department of Education, 1983.

Warmbrod, C., and Faddis, C. *Retraining and Upgrading Workers: A Guide for Postsecondary Educators.* Columbus: Ohio State University, National Center for Research in Vocational Education, 1983.

Warmbrod, C., Persavich, J., and L'Angelle, D. *Sharing Resources: Postsecondary Education and Industry Cooperation.* Research and Development Series No. 203. Columbus: Ohio State University, National Center for Research in Vocational Education, 1981.

Dorothy J. Kaplan is director of the business and industry programs at Northampton County Area Community College in Pennsylvania.

Material abstracted from recent additions to the Education Resources Information Center (ERIC) system provides further information on contracted instruction and other community college services to business and industry.

Sources and Information: The Community College Role in Economic and Labor-Force Development

Jim Palmer, Anita Colby, Diane Zwemer

Contracted instruction is one mechanism by which community colleges lend their expertise to area businesses and industries. Under the leadership of the American Association of Community and Junior Colleges, such college-industry collaborations have become a major theme of community college spokespersons. Indeed, many practitioners and administrators argue for an expanded community college role, one that makes the colleges not only a center for classroom instruction but also a partner with business and industry in a nationwide effort to foster economic recovery and growth.

The ERIC documents and journal articles cited in this chapter represent the growing literature on this proposed community college role. The citations, culled from a search of ERIC's *Resources in Education* and *Current Index to Journals in Education,* are grouped into five sections. Items in the first section discuss the broad topic of the community college role in labor-force and economic development. The second section

R. Kopecek, R. Clarke (Eds.). *Customized Job Training for Business and Industry.*
New Directions for Community Colleges, no. 48. San Francisco: Jossey-Bass, December 1984.

lists items dealing with college-business partnerships. These are followed, in the third section, by documents that examine college responses to changing technologies in the workplace. The last two sections list items that discuss employer needs assessment and contracted instruction.

Those items marked with an "ED" number are ERIC documents and can be ordered through the ERIC Document Reproduction Service (EDRS) in Alexandria, Virginia, or obtained on microfiche at over 650 libraries across the country. Those items without "ED" numbers are journal articles and are not available through EDRS; they must be obtained through regular library channels. For an EDRS order form and/or list of the libraries in your state that have ERIC microfiche collections, please write the ERIC Clearinghouse for Junior Colleges, 8118 Math-Sciences Building, UCLA, Los Angeles, California 90024.

The College Role in Labor-Force Development

Boyd-Beauman, F., and Piland, W. E. "Illinois, Arizona Find Great Resources in Colleges." *Community and Junior College Journal,* 1983, *54* (3), 18–20.

The authors review the findings of a study undertaken to determine the status of economic development programs within community colleges in Illinois and Arizona. The study revealed, among other findings, that most colleges take on the responsibilities of making initial contacts with area industries, developing specially designed training programs for those industries, and marketing college programs and services to the business community. The authors conclude with an outline of five strategies that should be included in college economic development plans.

Ellison, N. M. "BICCC: An Important Community College Initiative." Paper presented at the Business Industry Coalition seminar sponsored by the Kansas Association of Community Colleges, Topeka, January 24, 1983. 14 pp. (ED 227 891)

Ellison notes the variety of human resources development agencies that are involved in employment and job training efforts, describes the "Put America Back to Work" project of the American Association of Community and Junior Colleges, and argues for a strong role in the development of local business-industry councils (BICs). He stresses the importance of research and planning to the viability of BIC programs and argues that colleges will lose credibility if they do not take on a leadership role in cooperative efforts with business to promote human resource development.

Eskow, S. "The Community College and the Human Resources Development Council: Toward a National Training Strategy for the United States." Unpublished paper, 1982. 21 pp. (ED 238 459)

Noting the increased demand for technically trained workers in today's economy, Eskow argues that community colleges, more than any other public or private agency, are best suited to take on a leadership role in a national job development effort. To this end, he advocates the establishment of human resources development councils (HRDCs) at community colleges. Each HRDC would coordinate the efforts of industries, education, and government in developing technology transfer networks, providing job training programs, creating local economic development plans, and bringing new training resources into the community.

Eskow, S. "Putting America Back to Work: Phase II." *Community and Junior College Journal,* 1983, *54* (3), 12–14.

Eskow proposes a five-part agenda for phase II of the "Put America Back to Work" project, an effort undertaken by the American Association of Community and Junior Colleges to place two-year colleges at the forefront of a national job training strategy. The agenda calls on colleges to lead local forums or "town meetings" on economic development; to initiate cooperative efforts among business, government, and education; to provide leadership in the development of community economic development plans; to establish technology transfer networks; and to assess community education and training needs.

Mohn, M. (Ed.). *Primary Partners in Economic Development: Cooperation in High Technology—Community Colleges, Business and Industry, Labor and Government.* Conference proceedings, Seattle, Washington, August 20, 1982. Seattle, Wash.: Seattle Community College District, 1982. 112 pp. (ED 231 495)

These proceedings summarize the presentations made at a conference that was conducted, in part, to promote the state community college system as a primary vehicle for economic recovery. Individual presentations discuss cooperative programs between community colleges and industries in the state of Washington, the role of North Carolina community colleges in training workers for new and expanding industries in the state, and the role of community colleges in solving national economic problems. Viewpoints from business, industry, and government are represented.

Putting America Back to Work: A Concept Paper. Washington, D.C.: Amer-
can Association of Community and Junior Colleges, 1982. 12 pp.
(ED 214 577)

This paper notes the lack of a national policy on employment development and discusses the potential contribution of two-year colleges to a
national job training effort. These potential contributions are in areas
including training for specific occupations in industry; literacy education; the provision of assistance to operators of small businesses; and
the coordination of labor, education, and business organizations in
local economic development programs. The realization of these potential contributions, the authors argue, awaits only national leadership in
the establishment of a coordinated, nationwide approach to human
resources development.

Owen, H. J. "Program Planning for Economic Development in Community and Technical Colleges." *Community Services Catalyst,* 1983, *13*
(4), 18–23.

After describing North Carolina's commitment to economic development through the state's community and technical college system,
Owen details the role of the colleges in several labor-force development
efforts: cooperative skills training centers at which industries and colleges assess local training needs and develop needed programs; apprenticeship programs; a new and expanding industry program that provides new businesses with trained workers; in-plant skill training programs; and traditional vocational programs. The article concludes with
an outline of factors that testify to the success of North Carolina's economic development policies.

Tyree, L. W., and McConnell, N. C. *Linking Community Colleges with
Economic Development in Florida.* ISHE Fellows Program Research
Report No. 3. Tallahassee, Fla.: Institute for Studies in Higher
Education, 1982. 32 pp. (ED 226 785)

Drawing upon a review of the literature, the authors discuss the need
for increased cooperation between colleges and industry in labor-force
development, examine the role of state government in initiating and fos-
tering such cooperation, and describe the relationship between education
and industry in Florida. The report concludes with seven suggestions
for strengthening the community college role in future economic
development. These recommendations stress the need for strong government support for that role, improved assessment procedures that
document the effectiveness of college programs, the provision of training at the work site, and greater use of contracted training agreements.

College-Business Partnerships

Keyser, J., and Nicholson, R. S. "College/Chamber Synergy." *Community and Junior College Journal,* 1982-83, *53* (4), 38-39.

A discussion is provided of the relationship between Mount Hood Community College and the local chamber of commerce and their mutual interest in gaining improvements in the educational, social, and economic aspects of the community. The article highlights such programs as breakfast seminars, community leadership programs, international forum series, and a chamber-sponsored legislative activity, as well as the role these programs play in initating "a synergy which will strengthen both organizations and the communities served" (p. 39).

Learn, R. L. "A Comparison Between Business and Industry Linkage Structures in Pennsylvania Community and Junior Colleges and Those Described in the Literature." Unpublished master's thesis, Indiana University of Pennsylvania, 1983. 51 pp. (ED 230 253)

This research report details the methods and findings of a study conducted to compare and contrast the business and industry linkages highlighted in the community college literature with those in place in Pennsylvania's community and junior colleges. In addition to an extensive literature review, the report includes a discussion of the kinds of linkage programs currently operating in these institutions (for example, customized training programs, utilization of business and industry personnel, and practical work experience programs for students), the types of programs in existence in other states that are not being used in Pennsylvania (such as physical resource sharing); and the administrative and operational structures of the existing programs.

Parnell, D., and Yarrington, R. *Proven Partners: Business, Labor, and Community Colleges.* AACJC Pocket Reader 1. Washington, D.C.: American Association of Community and Junior Colleges, 1982. 59 pp. (ED 214 582)

This booklet provides brief descriptions of cooperative arrangements made by thirty-eight community colleges in twenty-three states with local businesses, industries, and labor unions in order to meet employee needs for training. The program descriptions include information on the nature of the program, problems to be addressed, types of courses and training provided, source of instructional staff, support services available, company contributions in terms of released time for employees, facilities, equipment, and funds, and the name of a contact person for further information.

Rinehart, R. L. "Industry-College Cooperation: New Components, Barriers, and Strategies." Paper presented at the annual convention of the American Association of Community and Junior Colleges, St. Louis, Mo., April 1982. 16 pp. (ED 215 739)

This paper describes a variety of linkage components that can help build and maintain effective relationships between the worlds of work and education. The paper examines (1) different forms of industry-education collaboration and their characteristics (for example, cooperative education, work study, apprenticeship, internship, and clinical experience programs); (2) potential problems and barriers to effective linkages (such as budget and cost factors, corporate and institutional policies, and legal restrictions); and (3) means of overcoming these barriers using problem-solving and group interaction skills.

College Responses to Advancing Technology

Barton, T. E., and others. *High-Technology Training at Greenville Technical College.* Greenville, S.C.: Greenville Technical College, 1984. 37 pp. (ED 242 380)

The three papers in this publication discuss the response of Greenville Technical College to advancing technology and the growing demand for technical training. Among other topics, the papers examine (1) the college's network of industry advisory councils; (2) the efforts made by the college to keep abreast of changing technologies in computerized metal cutting, microprocessors, computer electronics, programming, and office automation; and (3) the initiation of new programs in automated manufacturing engineering technology and in process control and instrumentation engineering technology.

Groff, W. H. "Assisting a College's Service Area in the Transition to the New Technology Society Through Strategic Planning and Management." Unpublished paper, 1983. 40 pp. (ED 231 453)

Noting the current change from a production-oriented economy to an information-oriented economy, Groff discusses a strategic planning and human resource development model used by North Central Technical College (Ohio) to keep abreast of technical advances and to assist its local service district in the adoption of new technologies. He then examines the role of the college in local economic renewal through involvement in such projects as the Ohio Technology Transfer Organization, which helps small businesses diagnose training needs.

Groff, W. H. "Computer Literacy: Data and Information Processing as the Core of the High-Technology Information Society." Paper presented at the 1982 Great Lakes Regional Conference of the American Technical Education Association, November 3–5, 1982. 20 pp. (ED 223 273)

After describing the efforts of North Central Technical College to project its data and word processing needs for the next several years and to implement an institutional commitment to computer literacy, this paper examines the implications of changing technologies for post-secondary education. Groff argues that colleges must do more than provide society with educated persons. Rather, he maintains, colleges must take a proactive role in facilitating a smooth changeover to the information age by identifying the technology needs of area industries, assisting those industries in the adoption of new technologies, and providing requisite personnel training.

Landrum, B., and Gluss, M. A. "Colleges Help Communities Vie for Payrolls." *Community and Junior College Journal,* 1983, *53* (7), 50–51.

Noting how the community college districts in Arizona operate as coordinators of vocational planning within each county, the authors outline the efforts of the Maricopa Community College District to meet the training requirements of high-technology firms in the Phoenix area. These efforts include district participation in the Arizona Association of Industrial Developers, customized training for area industries, a capital improvement plan for upgrading training facilities, and the formation of a high-technology industries advisory council. The article concludes with a discussion of the council's activities (including work opportunities that allow faculty to upgrade skills) and a checklist of steps to be taken in forming an advisory council.

Larkin, P. *Can Colleges and Universities Supply an Adequate Skilled Work-Force for Higher-Technology Needs in 1990? Problems, Prospects, and Policy for the Eighties.* Research Report No. 82-27. Largo, Md.: Prince Georges Community College, 1982. 21 pp. (ED 230 222)

Drawing upon an examination of Bureau of Labor Statistics forecasts and reviews of the numbers of college graduates in technical subject areas, this report examines the imbalance between the demand for technically trained personnel and the ability of higher education to supply technically trained graduates. In light of this imbalance, the author advocates increased state funding for high-technology education, increased efforts to improve mathematics and science education at the elementary and secondary levels, and the provision of flexible programs for adults who need to update their job skills.

Long, J. P. "Industry Speaks to Two-Year Colleges About High Technology." Unpublished paper, 1983, 8 pp. (ED 231 492)

This paper highlights the opinions, predictions, and suggestions of representatives from more than forty firms, who participated in a series of regional conferences sponsored by the National Postsecondary Alliance to inform college administrators about industry involvement in high technology and the role of two-year colleges in preparing students for technological jobs. The paper notes trends in (1) the role of industry, the military, and proprietary schools in technical training; (2) the role of computers, robotics, and semiconductors in high-technology development; (3) technical job opportunities in the health and communications fields; and (4) the production and distribution of software.

Lynch, E. "Macomb Community College Enters the World of High Tech." *VocEd*, 1982, *57* (7), 29–31.

Lynch outlines the responses of Macomb Community College (Michigan) to the growing need for technically trained workers in its service district and briefly describes the college's programs in interactive computer-aided design, robotics technology, and word and information processing. The success of each of these programs, the author notes, is based on the high budgetary commitment given to such programs and to faculty efforts to keep up to date with the latest technological innovations.

Moore, G. R. "Short-Term Training — Where the Action Is!" Unpublished paper, 1982. 9 pp. (ED 226 789)

This paper examines two short-term training programs undertaken by Chemeketa Community College (Oregon) to assist displaced workers in its local service district. The programs (which offer instruction in word processing, typing and transcribing, mobile home construction, electronic technology, computer operations, microcomputer repair, and computer-assisted graphics) focus on the acquisition of specific technical skills and minimize elective and general education course work. The author argues that the current movement toward an economy based on communications and high technologies will require community colleges to make short-term training a major part of their comprehensive curriculum.

Parsons, M. H. "Technology Transfer: Programs, Procedures, and Personnel." Paper presented at a round table at the annual convention of the American Association of Community and Junior Colleges, New Orleans, April 24–27, 1983. 9 pp. (ED 230 244)

After arguing the case for a strong community college role in transfering new technologies from the laboratory to practical applications in the workplace, Parsons discusses (1) different ways of implementing the technology transfer process, (2) the danger of attempting to transfer technologies that require prohibitively expensive changes in working conditions on equipment, and (3) barriers to technology transfer, such as high cost or a lack of expertise. The author draws upon the technology transfer efforts of Hagerstown Junior College (Maryland) for illustrative examples.

Rogers, R. H. *Landsat Technology Transfer to the Private and Public Sectors Through Community Colleges and Other Locally Available Institutions.* Phase III Program, Final Report. Ann Arbor, Mich.: Environmental Research Institute, 1982. 90 pp. (ED 229 065)

This report details the second-year outcomes of a program that investigated methods of making Landsat (satellite imagery) technology available to private-sector firms through a network consisting of the National Aeronautics and Space Administration (NASA), a university, a research institute, local community colleges, and private and public organizations. In the program, community colleges took on the responsibility for classifying neighborhood businesses in terms of technical or information needs, coordinating seminars for potential users and suppliers of Landsat data products, and serving as local contacts for technical assistance. The authors conclude that community colleges have the "commitment, expertise, and geographic distribution that is essential for effective transfer of . . . technologies" (p. 52).

The Role of SUNY's Community Colleges in Technical/Occupational Education. Analysis Paper No. 821. Albany: State University of New York, Office for Community Colleges, 1982. 18 pp. (ED 215 720)

Citing the increased demand for skilled employees in high-technology areas, this paper notes three methods used to finance the often expensive technical training programs offered by the two-year institutions of the State University of New York: (1) a funding formula providing colleges with bonus monies for students in business and technology programs that enhance the economic development of the state; (2) the provision of state funding for noncredit courses that are vocationally oriented; and (3) the provision of state aid for contract courses with business and industry. The bulk of the report lists occupational programs approved by SUNY since 1976.

Employer Needs Assessment

Allen, J. P. *Illinois Valley Industry Retention Program: Final Report.* Springfield: Illinois State Department of Commerce and Community Affairs; and Oglesby: Illinois Valley Community College, 1982. 42 pp. (ED 223 310)

This report describes the activities and outcomes of the Illinois Valley Industry Retention program, which involved representatives from the state government, Illinois Valley Community College, and local businesses in an effort to retain existing industries in the area and save presently available jobs for the area's citizens. The report highlights a study of local businesses and their site location, training needs, governmental assistance opportunities, suppliers, perceptions of the advantages and disadvantages of doing business in the state, and plans for expansion. In addition to study findings, the report presents recommendations reflecting industry concerns at the local, state, and federal levels, and it describes the survey instruments.

Future Skill Needs Assessment of Selected Metropolitan Milwaukee Business and Industry. Milwaukee, Wisc.: Human Resources Services and Milwaukee Area Technical College, Division of Economic Development, 1983. 87 pp. (ED 235 869)

Prepared as part of a research project conducted to identify the skills that will be needed by businesses and industry in Milwaukee within the next five to ten years, this report presents the views of industry representatives regarding recent changes in the knowledge and skills necessary to job performance, existing skill deficiencies in current employees or job applicants, and new skills and jobs that will be required in the future. The study's findings underscore the difficulty of projecting future needs due to the rapid technological changes, employers' dissatisfaction with the basic educational skills of prospective employees, the importance of computer skills, and the prospect of increasing competition between two- and four-year college graduates.

Lyons, D. "Humboldt County Employer Survey." Report prepared as part of the Humboldt County Labor Market Information Project and financed under the provisions of Title VII of the Comprehensive Employment and Training Act of 1973, 1981. 139 pp. (ED 223 276)

This report details the findings of a study conducted in Humboldt County to assess the employment needs and requirements of large and small businesses in the area. The report contains profiles of local businesses, information on their familiarity with regional employment programs, profiles of the entry-level positions within the firms, their experiences with hiring personnel through employment and training programs and the performance of these employees, and the kinds of ongoing staff development and continuing education programs offered through the firms.

Stoehr, K. W., and Banerdt, J. *Walworth County Employer Needs Assessment Study.* Kenosha, Wisc.: Gateway Technical Institute, 1983. 43 pp. (ED 229 097)

Findings and recommendations are presented from a study conducted by Gateway Technical Institute (GTI) to obtain information from local businesses and industry regarding special high-technology training needs, plans for expansion, on-site training, interest in cooperative training programs with GTI, evaluation of GTI-trained personnel, and other characteristics. The study revealed that, while one-third of the employers planned to expand, nearly half had no plans for expansion; tuition reimbursement, in-house training, and release time were the most frequently cited means of encouraging employees to improve their skills; and almost half were interested in implementing supervisory training programs with GTI assistance. The questionnaire is included with the study report.

Williamson, D. B. *Research Findings of Employer Needs Assessment Survey.* Florence, S.C.: Florence-Darlington Technical College, 1981. 63 pp. (ED 224 518)

This report presents findings and recommendations from a study conducted by Florence-Darlington Technical College (FDTC). The study gathered information on the training needs of local employers, discrepancies between employment needs and college programs, and employers' perceptions of educational priorities. Study findings, based on responses from 121 local firms, indicated that, though most employers seldom or never employed FDTC graduates, they were willing to do so and felt employment opportunities with their firms were good. They indicated that graduates needed good safety habits and the ability to operate and take care of equipment.

106

Contract Education

Brown, S. M. *A Primer for Colleges Who Intend to Provide Training in Industry.* Haverhill, Mass.: Northern Essex Community College; and Boston: Massachusetts State Commission on Postsecondary Education, 1981. 22 pp. (ED 210 069)

Based on experiences at Northern Essex Community College, this paper describes a basic process for the development of community college programs to provide training for local business and industry. The paper outlines steps in starting a training program, different approaches for contacting business, and the process involved in designing a program to meet the company's training needs. Elements necessary for the program proposal are discussed, as well as issues to be considered in proposal design and negotiation. A model for student follow-up and various funding models are explained.

Gold, C. L. *Contracting with Business and Industry: Use Your Community Resources.* Escanaba, Mich.: Bay de Noc Community College, 1982. 30 pp. (ED 226 768)

A description is provided of Bay de Noc Community College's Contracting with Business and Industry program, a low-cost, interdisciplinary career training program for nontraditional students. The report describes how, through contracts between the college and local businesses, students acquire on-the-job training while participating in on-campus classes to develop skills in job interviewing, interpersonal relations, resumé preparation, the American enterprise system, and attitude training. The report discusses the program's rationale and assesses its effectiveness and outcomes. A summary of program costs is appended.

Hodgin, R. F. *A Cost-Benefit Analysis for Seafood-Processing Training Sessions in the Galveston Bay Area.* Texas City, Tex.: College of the Mainland; and Austin: Texas Education Agency, 1982. 35 pp. (ED 216 745)

This report details the assumptions, limitations, procedures, and findings of a cost-benefit study of training sessions for seafood processors offered by the College of the Mainland in Texas. Data collected from the college and local companies participating in the program, federal and state records and statistics, and direct observation revealed that, for every dollar invested by the state in the training program, $1.83 was returned, largely through increased sales tax revenues. The report includes a descriptive history of the Texas seafood harvesting and processing industries, which discusses price fluctuations, seasonality, and labor-force needs; statistics on wages; and fishing regulations.

Mahoney, J. R. *Community College Centers for Contracted Programs: A Sequel to Shoulders to the Wheel.* Washington, D.C.: American Association of Community and Junior Colleges and United States Department of Energy, 1982. 77 pp. (ED 229 061)

Based on a survey of thirty-seven community colleges, this booklet summarizes the characteristics of special community college centers that provide educational services to business, industry, government, and other local community groups on a contract basis. This booklet provides (1) a discussion of factors that have influenced the creation of such centers; (2) a composite description of the centers' goals, objectives, services, contact and linkage approaches, program development procedures, and administrative details; (3) a review of problems experienced by the centers; (4) advice on initiating such programs offered by survey respondents; and (5) case studies of twelve such centers.

Jim Palmer is a staff writer at the ERIC Clearinghouse for Junior Colleges in Los Angeles.

Anita Colby is the documents coordinator at the ERIC Clearinghouse for Junior Colleges in Los Angeles.

Diane Zwemer is the user services librarian at the ERIC Clearinghouse for Junior Colleges in Los Angeles.

Index